EVERYDAY SCIENCE MYSTERIES

STORIES FOR INQUIRY-BASED SCIENCE TEACHING

EVERYDAY SCIENCE MYSTERIES

STOries FOr INQUIrY-BASED SCIENCE Teaching

Richard Konicek-Moran, Ed.D.
Professor Emeritus
University of Massachusetts
Amherst

Foreword by Page Keeley

NSTApress
National Science Teachers Association

National Science Teachers Association

Claire Reinburg, Director
Judy Cusick, Senior Editor
Andrew Cocke, Associate Editor
Betty Smith, Associate Editor

ART AND DESIGN
Will Thomas, Jr., Director
Tim French, Senior Graphic Designer (cover, interior design, illustrations)

PRINTING AND PRODUCTION
Catherine Lorrain, Director

NATIONAL SCIENCE TEACHERS ASSOCIATION
Gerald F. Wheeler, Executive Director
David Beacom, Publisher

Library of Congress Cataloging-in-Publication Data
Konicek-Moran, Richard.
  Everyday science mysteries : stories for inquiry-based science teaching / by Richard Konicek-Moran ; foreword by Page Keeley.
     p. cm.
  Includes index.
  ISBN 978-1-93353-121-2
  1. Science--Methodology. 2. Problem solving. 3. Science--Study and teaching. 4. Science--Miscellanea. 5. Detective and mystery stories.
I. Title.
Q175.3.K663 2008
372.35'044--dc22
                         2008004614

  eISBN 978-1-935155-60-7

NSTA is committed to publishing material that promotes the best in inquiry-based science education. However, conditions of actual use may vary, and the safety procedures and practices described in this book are intended to serve only as a guide. Additional precautionary measures may be required. NSTA and the authors do not warrant or represent that the procedures and practices in this book meet any safety code or standard of federal, state, or local regulations. NSTA and the authors disclaim any liability for personal injury or damage to property arising out of or relating to the use of this book, including any of the recommendations, instructions, or materials contained therein.

CONTENTS

The Stories and Background Material for Teachers

acknowledgments

This book is dedicated to my wife, Kathleen, my most critical editor and best friend and to Page Keeley, my muse, without whose help and encouragement, it would not have been published.

I would like to thank the following teachers and administrators who have helped me by field-testing the stories and ideas contained in this book over many years. Without their help, criticism, and encouragement, I would never have had the opportunity to work with such dedicated educators.

I cannot express enough, my thanks to the following educators who have been my support over the last 50 years in one way or another and helped me, through trials, to believe that these stories and inquiry really works in schools with real children.

Kathy Davis,
    University of Massachussetts Amherst
Richard Haller
Jo Ann Hurley
Linda Denault
Lore Knaus
Theresa Williamson
Dr. Terez Waldoch,
    Principal, Wildwood Elementary, Amherst
Third Grade Team at Burgess Elementary,
    Sturbridge, MA
Second grade Team at Burgess Elementary
    at Sturbridge, MA
Justin Konicek and my son Tim Konicek
    who helped me develop the moon model
Alesia Peck
Teachers at Millbury, MA, Elementary Schools
Former UMass doctoral students
Diana Campbell
Barbara La Corte
Betsy Koscher
Wanita Lafond

All teachers in my graduate and undergraduate classes who wrote stories and tried them in their classes and tried my stories in their classes.

To Dr. Bob Barkman of Springfield College in Massachusetts who supported me and used the stories and techniques in workshops with Springfield elementary and middle school teachers.

To my advisor at Columbia University, the late Professor Willard Jacobson, who made it possible for me to find my place in teacher education at the university level.

I also wish to thank Skip Snow, Lori Oberhofer, Jeff Kline, and all of the biologists in the Everglades National Park with whom I have had the pleasure of working for the past seven years for helping me to remember how to be a scientist again. And to the interpretation group in the Everglades National Park, Katie Bliss, Maria Thompson, Laurie Humphry, and all of the other interpreters who helped me to realize again that it is possible to help someone to look without telling them what to see.

My thanks to Bob Samples and Cheryl Charles for showing me another part of education in creativity that I had forgotten was part of me.

Last but not least are the following graduate students who helped me field test the book and stories in a class entitled *Exploring the Natural Sciences Through Inquiry*, which used the book in an entirely different way, as an adult guide to learning content.

Brittany Baumann
Beth Silverman
Christine Anderson
Renee Mackay
John Broomwald

But my most sincere thanks goes to Claire Reinburg of NSTA who had the faith in my work to publish it and to Andrew Cocke my editor who helped me through the final steps.

Also to the peer reviewers for their fine reviews of the material and for their very helpful suggestions for improving the final product.

Foreword

Several years ago I had the pleasure of meeting the author, Richard Konicek-Moran, at a presentation I gave in Lexington, Massachusetts. When I heard that "Dr. Konicek" was registered for the conference, I was quite excited—little did Dick know at that time that I regarded him as my "muse." Dick was the inspiration for my work on probing students' ideas in science, which eventually led to the publication of the NSTA best-selling series *Uncovering Student Ideas in Science.*

I was first introduced to Dick's work in inquiry and conceptual change teaching almost two decades ago as a classroom teacher when I participated in the first *Private Universe* live video telecast in which Dick presented children's ideas about light and constructivist teaching and learning. Also, in the early 1990s I read his Kappan article *Teaching for Conceptual Change: Confronting Children's Experience* (Watson and Konicek 1990). The article was about a study conducted in a classroom of Massachusetts fourth graders who were exploring the topic of heat. Their teacher artfully probed the students' ideas and found that students believed that the hats and sweaters they wore to keep warm in the winter generated their own heat. They thought even rugs got "wicked hot."

Sensing their naïve conceptions, the teacher gave them an opportunity to test their ideas by placing thermometers in hats, sweaters, and even a rolled up rug. When the first experiment revealed that the temperature reading on the thermometers failed to rise, students were convinced that they needed to leave the thermometers in longer. They left the thermometers in overnight and came back the next day convinced the temperatures would be soaring! Lo and behold, they still found no demonstrable change. However, they still weren't ready to abandon their strongly held ideas. The teacher could have stopped at that point, corrected the students, explained the reason why the temperature did not go up, and moved on. But no, this talented teacher enabled students to "own the problem" and continue pondering, testing, and discussing their ideas until they were ready to give up their erroneous belief and incorporate new knowledge that allowed them to construct a scientific understanding, appropriate for their developmental level.

Dick's article inspired me to come up with intriguing questions for students and eventually led to my development of "The Mitten Problem" probe published in *Uncovering Student Ideas in Science: 25 Formative Assessment Probes* (vol. 1) (Keeley, Eberle, and Farrin 2005). The rest is history as more than 75 of these probes have been published and are now being used by thousands of teachers all over the country. I can honestly say that Dick's article lit the spark that put me on the path of publishing the probing questions I had developed over the years and continue to develop in order to build teacher's capacity to use intriguing questions and contexts to learn more about their students' conceptions and engage them in thinking through, discussing, and testing ideas they "owned."

What does this have to do with *Everyday Science Mysteries?* Well, the tables had turned and now it was my turn to act as a muse to see Dick's innovative idea of making science mystery stories accessible to teachers everywhere come to fruition. Dick and I had a wonderful conversation about the connection between the formative assessment probe work I was doing and the similar work he was doing with children's science mystery stories he had written over the years. We recognized the complementary nature of our work and what a significant contribution to teaching and learning he could make by publishing these stories through NSTA Press. Like the probes in *Uncovering Student Ideas,* the mystery stories present real problems set in everyday contexts for students to think through, test their ideas, and come up with their own explanations. Like the probes, the mystery stories are built on the hallmark of good inquiry-based teaching and constructivist learning. They allow students to "own" both the question and the solution. Teachers can step back and observe and facilitate children's learning, and in the process, learn a lot about teaching and learning.

As we "mused" over the potential of this book to positively impact elementary and middle school students' opportunities to learn, I realized Dick's vision for this book and its use go well beyond contributing interesting stories to promote student thinking and engage students in real inquiry. It also serves as a teacher-friendly reference on conceptual change teaching connected to important learning goals reflected in state and national standards. It raises teachers' awareness of the research on children's commonly held ideas in science so that they might anticipate their own students' having similar ideas. The explanation of the science behind each story helps teachers improve their own content knowledge and connects it to pedagogical strategies and activities they can use to help students build their conceptual understanding. With the increasing emphasis on reading and literacy in response to No Child Left Behind, this book presents a meaningful way to incorporate literacy into children's science experiences. I am proud to know Dick as one of my fellow NSTA Press Authors.

What makes this book so special is the unique way science is integrated into the storyline, using characters and situations children can easily identify with. The student is brought right into the story and is invited to think about his or her own ideas and how they compare to the characters'. Real science is at the core as students take on the task of finishing the story by designing and carrying out their own investigations to test their ideas, make sense of the problem, and devise explanations.

Eleanor Duckworth once said, "The having of wonderful ideas is what I consider the essence of intellectual development" (1996, p. 1). "The more we help children to have their wonderful ideas and to feel good about themselves for having them, the more likely it is that they will some day happen upon wonderful ideas that no one else has happened upon before" (1996, p. 14). These stories are bound to reveal the wonderful ideas all students have, give them the confidence to explore their own thinking, and provide opportunities for them to "do" science rather than have science "done to them." Perhaps some day these young science mystery story solvers will be our next generation of scientists who will pursue their wonderful ideas to help solve the science mysteries that continue to build our understanding of the world we live in. Thank you Dick, for having the "wonderful ideas" that led to this book!

Page Keeley
NSTA President 2008–09

references

Duckworth, E. 1996. *The having of wonderful ideas and other essays on teaching and learning.* NY: Teachers College Press.

Keeley, P., F. Eberle, and L. Farrin. 2005. *Uncovering student ideas in science: 25 formative assessment probes* (vol. 1). Arlington, VA: NSTA Press.

Watson, B., and R. Konicek. May 1990. Teaching for conceptual change: Confronting children's experience. *Phi Delta Kappan* 680–684.

Preface

In the mid-1990s, at the second Misconceptions Conference at Cornell University in Ithaca, New York, I distinctly remember having a conversation with Dr. James Shymansky, then at the University of Iowa, now at the University of Missouri in St. Louis. There, far above Cayuga's waters, we talked about an idea he espoused. The idea was for a new type of literature. He complained that current literature, for the most part, merely told children what scientists had found out about certain phenomena and left out the drama of discovery and trial and failure. For this conversation and ideas gleaned from it, I offer heartfelt thanks.

Dr. Shymansky suggested that the current children's literature served a valuable purpose, but could also be written so that it offered a challenge to students and a skilled teacher could use such literature to parlay this challenge into classroom inquiry. He offered examples of such literature in the form of stories that would capture children's interests and leave the solution in their hands, rather than solve the challenge for them.

This encounter had a profound effect upon me and I immediately went back to the University of Massachusetts and began to explore these possibilities with graduate students in my elementary science methods class. We selected science topics, wrote stories about phenomena, and added challenges by leaving the endings open, requiring the readers to engage in what we hoped would be actual inquiry in order to finish the story.

Over the course of the semester we wrote many stories and the graduate students tried them out with students in their classrooms. The children enjoyed the stories and we learned some important lessons on how to formulate stories so they provided the proper challenge.

For years afterward, I used the idea with my graduate and undergraduate students in the elementary science methods classes. In lieu of the usual lesson plan my class requirements included an assignment that asked them to write a story about a science phenomenon and include a follow-up paper that described how they would use the story to encourage inquiry learning in their classrooms. As I learned more about the concept, I was able to add techniques to my own repertoire, which enhanced the quality of the stories and follow-up papers.

I learned that student teachers benefit from talking about their stories with other students and their instructor. They can gain valuable feedback before they launch into the final story. We organized small group meetings of no more than five students to preview and discuss ideas. We also designed a checklist, which helped to clarify the basic ideas behind the concept of the "challenge story." See below.

Things to think about as you write your story

Does your story…

(1) address a single concept or conceptual scheme?

(2) address a topic of interest to your target age group?

(3) try to provide your audience with a problem they can solve through direct activity?

(4) require the students to become actively involved—hands-on, minds-on?

(5) have a real open-ended format?

(6) provide enough information for the students to identify and attack the problem?

(7) consider whether materials you intend for the students to use are readily available to them?

(8) provide opportunities for students to discuss the story and come up with a plan for finding some answers?

(9) make data collection and analysis of those data a necessity?

(10) provide some way for you to assess what their current preconceptions are about the topic? (This can be implicit or explicit.)

As always, practice makes for a better product and eventually my students were producing stories which were both useful for them in their classes and acceptable to me as a form of assessment of their learning about teaching science.

As the years went by, teachers began to ask me if my own stories I used for examples in class were available for them to use. They encouraged me to publish them in a book. So here it is. I hope that it will provide you with ideas and inspiration to develop more inquiry oriented lessons in your classrooms. And perhaps you may be motivated to try writing your own stories for teaching those concepts you find most difficult to get across to students.

INTRODUCTION
CASE STUDIES ON HOW TO USE THE STORIES IN THE CLASSROOM

To open this book, I would like to introduce you to one of the stories and then show how it was used by two teachers: Teresa, a second-grade teacher and Lore, a fifth-grade teacher. Then in the following chapters I will explain the philosophy and organization of the book before going to the stories and background material. Please go to page 39 and read the story "Where Are the Acorns?" before continuing.

HOW TWO TEACHERS USED "WHERE ARE THE ACORNS?"

Teresa, a veteran second-grade teacher

Teresa usually begins the school year with a unit on fall and change. This year she looked at the National Science Education Standards (NSES) and decided that a unit on the sky and cyclic changes would be in order. Since shadows were something that the children often noticed and included in playground games (shadow tag), Teresa thought using the story of "Cheeks" the squirrel would be appropriate.

To begin, she felt that it was extremely important to know what the children already knew about the Sun and the shadows cast from objects. She wanted to know what kind of knowledge they shared with Cheeks and what kind of knowledge they had that the story's hero did not have. She arranged the children in a circle so that they could see each other and hear each other's comments. Teresa read the story to them, stopping along the way to see that they knew that Cheeks had made the decision on where to bury the acorns during the late summer and that the squirrel was looking for her buried food during the winter. She asked them to tell her what they thought they knew about the shadows that Cheeks had seen. She labeled a piece of chart paper, "Our Best Ideas So Far." As

they told her what they "knew," she recorded their statements in their own words:

- "Shadows change every day."
- "Shadows are longer in winter."
- "Shadows are shorter in winter."
- "Shadows get longer every day."
- "Shadows get shorter every day."
- "Shadows don't change at all."
- "Shadows aren't out every day."
- "Shadows move when you move."

She asked the students if it was okay to add a word or two to each of their statements so they could test them out. She turned their statements into questions and the list then looked like this:

- "Do shadows change every day?"
- "Are shadows longer in winter?"
- "Are shadows shorter in winter?"
- "Do shadows get longer every day?"
- "Do shadows get shorter every day?"
- "Do shadows change at all?"
- "Are shadows out every day?"
- "Do shadows move when you move?"

Teresa focused the class on the questions that could help solve Cheeks' dilemma. The children picked "Are shadows longer or shorter in the winter?" and "Do shadows change at all?" The children were asked to make predictions based on their experience. Some said that the shadows would get longer as we moved toward winter and some predicted the opposite. Even though there was a question as to whether they would change at all, they agreed unanimously that there would probably be some change over time. If they could get data to support that there was change, that question would be removed from the chart.

Now the class had to find a way to answer their questions and test predictions. Teresa helped them talk about fair tests and asked them how they might go about answering the questions. They agreed almost at once that they should measure the shadow of a tree each day and write it down and should use the same tree and measure the shadow every day at the same time. They weren't sure why time was important except that they said they wanted to make sure everything was fair. Even though data about all of the questions would be useful, Teresa thought that at this stage, looking for more than one type of data might be overwhelming for her children.

Teresa checked the terrain outside and realized that the shadows of most trees might get so long during the winter months that they would touch one of the buildings and become difficult to measure. That could be a learning experience but at the same time it would frustrate the children to have their investigation ruined after months of work. She decided to try to convince the children to use an artificial "tree" that was small enough to avoid our concern. To her surprise, there was no objection to substituting an artificial tree since, "If we measured that same tree every day, it would still be fair." She made a tree out of a dowel that was about 15 cm tall and the children insisted that they glue a triangle on the top to make it look more like a tree.

The class went outside as a group and chose a spot where the sun shone without obstruction and took a measurement. Teresa was concerned that her students were not yet adept at using rulers and tape measures so she had the children measure the length of the shadow from the base of the tree to its tip with a piece of yarn and then glued that yarn onto a wall chart above the date when the measurement was taken. The children were delighted with this.

For the first week, teams of three went out and took daily measurements. By the end of the week, Teresa noted that the day-to-day differences were so small that perhaps they should consider taking a measurement once a week. This worked much better, as the chart was less "busy" but still showed any important changes that might happen.

As the weeks progressed, it became evident that the shadow was indeed getting longer each week. Teresa talked with the students about what would make a shadow get longer and armed with flashlights, the children were able to make longer shadows of pencils by lowering the flashlight. The Sun must be getting lower too if this was the case, and this observation was added to the chart of questions. Later, Teresa wished that she had asked the children to keep individual science notebooks so that she could have been more aware of how each individual child was viewing the experiment.

The yarn chart showed the data clearly and the only question seemed to be, "How long will the shadow get?" Teresa revisited the Cheeks story and the children were able to point out that Cheeks' acorns were probably much closer to the tree than the winter shadows indicated. Teresa went on with another unit on fall changes and each week added another piece of yarn to the chart. She was relieved that she could carry on two science units at once and still capture the children's interest about the investigation each week after the measurement. After winter break, there was great excitement when the shadow began getting shorter. The shortening actually began at winter solstice around December 21 but the children were on break until after New Year's. Now, the questions became "Will it keep getting shorter? For how long?" Winter passed and spring came and finally the end of the school year was approaching. Each week, the measurements were taken and each week a discussion was held on the meaning of the data. The chart was full of yarn strips and the pattern was obvious. The fall of last year had produced longer and longer shadow measurements until the New Year and then the shadows had begun to get shorter. "How short will they get?" and "Will they get down to nothing?" questions were added to the chart. During the last week of school, they talked about their conclusions and the children were convinced that the Sun was lower and cast longer shadows during the fall to winter time and that after the new year, the Sun got higher in the sky and made the shadows shorter. They were also aware that the seasons were changing and that the higher Sun seemed to mean warmer weather and trees producing leaves. The students were ready to think about seasonal changes in the sky and relating them to seasonal cycles. At least Teresa thought they were.

On the final meeting day in June, she asked her students what they thought the shadows would look like next September. After a great deal of thinking, they agreed that since the shadows were getting so short that by next September, they would be gone or so short that they would be hard to measure. Oh my!! The idea of a cycle had escaped them, and no wonder, since it hadn't really been discussed. The obvious extrapolation of the chart would indicate that the trend of shorter shadows would continue. Teresa knew that she would not have a chance to continue the investigation next September but she might talk to the third-grade team and see if they would at least carry it on for a few weeks so that the children could see the repeat of the previous September data. Then the students might be ready to think more about seasonal changes and certainly their experience would be useful in the upper grades where seasons and the reasons for seasons would become a curricular issue. Despite these shortcomings, it was a marvelous experience and the children were given a great opportunity to design an investigation and collect data to answer their questions about the squirrel story at a level appropriate to their development. Teresa felt that the children had an opportunity to carry out a long-term investigation, gather data, and come up with conclusions along the way about Cheeks' dilemma. She felt also that the standard had been partially met or at least was in progress. She would talk with the third-grade team about that.

Lore (pronounced Laurie), a fifth-grade veteran teacher

In September while working in the school, I had gone to Lore's fifth-grade class for advice. I read them the Cheeks story and asked them at which grade they thought it would be most appropriate. They agreed that it would most likely fly best at second grade. It seemed, with their advice, that Teresa's decision to use it there was a good one.

However, about a week after Teresa began to use the story, I received a note from Lore, telling me that her students were asking her all sorts of questions about shadows, the Sun, and the seasons, and could I help. Despite their insistence that the story belonged in the second grade, the fifth graders were intrigued enough by the story to begin asking questions about shadows. We

now had two classes interested in Cheeks' dilemma but at two different developmental levels. The fifth graders were asking questions about daily shadows, direction of shadows, and seasonal shadows and they were asking, "Why is this happening?" Lore wanted to use an inquiry approach to help them find answers to their questions but needed help. Even though the Cheeks story had opened the door to their curiosity, we agreed that perhaps a story about a pirate burying treasure in the same way Cheeks had buried acorns might be better suited to the fifth-grade interests in the future.

Lore looked at the NSES for her grade level and saw that they called for observing and describing the Sun's location and movements and studying natural objects in the sky and their patterns of movement. But the students' questions, we felt, should lead the investigations. Lore was intrigued by the 5E approach to enquiry (*engage, elicit, explore, explain, and evaluate*) so since the students were already "engaged," she added the "elicit" phase to find out what her students already knew. So, Lore started her next class asking the class what they "knew" about the shadows that Cheeks used and what caused them. The students stated:

> "Shadows are long in the morning, short at midday and longer again in the afternoon."
> "There is no shadow at noon because the Sun is directly overhead."
> "Shadows are in the same place every day so we can tell time by them."
> "Shadows are shorter in the summer than in the winter."
> "You can put a stick in the ground and tell time by its shadow."

Just as Teresa had done, Lore changed these statements to questions, and they entered the "exploration" phase of the 5E inquiry method.

Luckily, Lore's room opened out onto a grassy area that was always open to the Sun. The students made boards that were 30 cm square and drilled holes in the middle and put a toothpick in the hole. They attached paper to the boards and drew shadow lines every half hour on the paper. They brought them in each afternoon and discussed their results. There were many discussions about whether or not it made a difference where they placed their boards from day to day.

They were gathering so much data that it was becoming cumbersome. One student suggested that they use overhead transparencies to record shadow data and then overlay them to see what kind of changes occurred. Everyone agreed that it was a great idea.

Lore introduced the class to the *Old Farmer's Almanac* and the tables of sunsets, sunrises, and lengths of days. This led to an exciting activity one day that involved math. Lore asked them to look at the sunrise time and sunset time on one given day and to calculate the length of the daytime sun hours. Calculations went on for a good ten minutes and Lore asked each group to demonstrate how they had calculated the time to the class. There must have been at least six different methods used and most of them came up with a common answer. The students were amazed that so many different methods could produce the same answer. They also agreed that several of the methods were more efficient than others and finally agreed that using a 24-hour clock method was the easiest. Lore was ecstatic that they had created so many methods and was convinced that their understanding of time was enhanced by this revelation.

This also showed that children are capable of metacognition—thinking about their thinking. Research (Metz 1995) tells us that elementary students are not astute at thinking about the way they reason but that they can learn to do so through practice and encouragement. Metacognition is important if students are to engage in inquiry. They need to understand how they process information and how they learn. In this particular instance, Lore had the children explain how they came to their solution for the length of day problem so that they could be more aware of how they went about solving the challenge. Students can also learn about their thinking processes from peers who are more likely to be at the same developmental level. Discussions in small groups or as an entire class can provide opportunities for the teacher to probe for more depth in student explanations. The teacher can ask the students who explain their technique to be more specific about how they used their thought processes: dead ends as well as successes. Students can also learn more about their metacognitive processes by writing in their notebooks about how they thought through their problem and found a solution. Talking about their thinking or explaining their methods of problem solving in writing can lead to a better understanding of how they can use reasoning skills better in future situations.

I should mention here that Lore went on to teach other units in science while the students continued to gather their data. She would come back to the unit periodically for a day or two so the children could process their findings. After a few months, the students were ready to get some help in finding a model that explained their data. Lore gave them globes and clay so that they could place their observers at their latitude on the globe. They used flashlights to replicate their findings. Since all globes are automatically tilted at a 23.5-degree angle it raised the question as to why globes were made that way. It was time for the "explanation" part of the lesson and Lore helped them to see how the tilt of the Earth could help them to make sense of their experiences with the shadows and the Sun's apparent motion in the sky.

The students made posters explaining how the seasons could be explained by the tilt of the Earth and the Earth's revolution around the Sun each year. They had "evaluated" their understanding and "extended" it beyond their experience. It was, Lore agreed, a very successful "6E" experience. It had included the engage and elicit, explore, explain, evaluate, and the added extend phase.

references

Metz, K. E. 1995. Reassessment of developmental constraints on children's science instruction. *Review of Educational Research* 65 (2): 93–127.

Yankee Publishing. *The old farmer's almanac,* published yearly since 1792. Dublin, NH: Author.

CHAPTER 1

THEORY BEHIND THE BOOK

We have all heard people refer to any activity that takes place in a science lesson as an "experiment." Yet, as taught today, science is practically devoid of true experiments. Experiments by definition test hypotheses, which are also usually absent from school science. A hypothesis is a human creation developed by a person who has been immersed in a problem for a sufficient amount of time to feel the need to propose an explanation for an event or situation over which he or she has been puzzled.

However, it is quite common and proper for us to investigate our questions without hypotheses. Investigations can be carried out as "fair tests," which are possibly more appropriate for elementary classrooms, because children often have not had the experience of prior research to set up a hypothesis in the true scientific mode. A hypothesis is more than a guess. A hypothesis will most often have an " if…then…" statement in it. For example, "*If* I place mealworm larvae in the refrigerator, *then* they will develop more slowly than those in a warm environment." Predictions in school science should also be more than mere guesses or hunches, however. Predictions should be based upon experience and thoughtful consideration. Regularly asking children to give reasons for their predictions is a good way to help them to see the difference between guessing and predicting.

Two elements are often missing in most school science curricula: *sufficient time* to puzzle over problems and problems that have some *real-life application*. It is much more likely that students will "cover" in a prescribed time period an area of study, say, pond life, with readings, demonstrations, and a field trip to a pond with an expert, topped off with individual or group reports on various pond animals and plants, complete with shoebox

dioramas and giant posters. Or there may be a study of the solar system with reports on facts about the planets, complete with dioramas and culminating with a class model of the solar system hung from the ceiling.

These lessons are naturally fun to do, but the problem is that they seldom pose any real problems; nothing into which the students can sink their collective teeth, use their minds, ponder, puzzle, hypothesize, and then experiment.

You have certainly noticed that most science curricula have a series of "critical" activities in which students participate and which supposedly lead to an understanding of a particular concept. In most cases, there is an assumption that students share a common view or a common set of preconceptions about the concept so that the activities will move the students collectively from one point to another, hopefully closer to the accepted scientific view. This is a particularly dangerous assumption since research shows us that students enter into learning situations with a variety of preconceptions. These preconceptions are not only well ingrained in the students' minds but are exceptionally resistant to change. Going through the series of prescribed activities will have little meaning to students who have brought to the lessons conceptions that have little connection to the planned lessons.

Bonny Shapiro, in her book, *What Children Bring to Light* (1994), points out in indisputable detail how a well-meaning science teacher ran his students through a series of activities on the nature of light without knowing that the students in the class all shared the misconception that seeing any object originates in the eye of the viewer and not from the reflection of light from an object into the eye. The activities were, for all intents and purposes, wasted, although the students had "solved the teacher" (rather than the problems) to the extent that they were able to fill in the worksheets and pass the test at the end of the unit—all the while doubting the critical concept that light reflecting from object to eye was the paramount fact and meaning of the act of seeing. "Solving the teacher" means that the children have learned a teacher's mannerisms, techniques, speech patterns, and perhaps teaching methods to the point that they can predict exactly what the teacher wants, what pleases her or annoys her, and how they can perform so that the teacher believes they have learned and understood what she expected of them.

Eleanor Duckworth, in her monograph *Inventing Density* (1986), says, "The critical experiments themselves cannot impose their own meanings. One has to have done a major part of the work already, one has to have developed a network of ideas in which to imbed the experiments."

So, how does a teacher make sure that her students develop a network of ideas in which to embed such activities? How does the teacher uncover student preconceptions about the topic to be studied? I believe that this book can offer some answers to these questions and offer some suggestions for remedying the problems mentioned above.

What Is Inquiry Anyway?

There is probably no one definition of "teaching for inquiry," but at this time the acknowledged authorities on this topic are the National Research Council (NRC) and the American Association for the Advancement of Science (AAAS). After all, they are respectively the authors of the *National Science Education Standards* and the *Benchmarks for Science Literacy,* upon which most states have based their curriculum standards. For this reason, I will use their definition, which I will follow throughout the book. The NRC, in *Inquiry and the National Science Education Standards: A Guide for Teaching and Learning* (2000), says that in order for real inquiry to take place in the classroom, the following five essentials must occur. They are:

(1) Learner engages in scientifically oriented questions.
(2) Learner gives priority to evidence in responding to questions.
(3) Learner formulates explanations from evidence.
(4) Learner connects explanations to scientific knowledge.
(5) Learner communicates and justifies explanations. (p. 29)

In essence, the NRC strives to encourage more learner self-direction and less direction from the teacher as time goes on during the school years. They also make it very clear that all science cannot be taught in this fashion. Science teaching that uses a variety of strategies is less apt to bore students and will be more effective. Giving demonstrations, leading discussions, solving presented problems, and entering into a productive discourse about science are all viable alternatives. However, the NRC does suggest that certain common components should be shared by whichever instructional model is used. These are:

(1) Students engage with a scientific question, event, or phenomenon. This connects with what they already know, creates dissonance with their own ideas, and/or motivates them to learn more.

(2) Students explore ideas though hands-on experiences, formulate and test hypotheses, solve problems, and create explanations for what they observe.

(3) Students analyze and interpret data, synthesize their ideas, build models, and clarify concepts and explanations with teachers and other sources of scientific knowledge.

(4) Students extend their new understanding and abilities and apply what they have learned to new situations.

(5) Students, with their teachers, review and assess what they have learned and how they have learned it. (p. 35)

The Reasons for This Book

According to a summary of current thinking in science education in the journal *Science Education,* "one result seems to be consistently demonstrated: students leave science classes with more positive attitudes about science (and their concepts of themselves as science participants) when they learn science through inductive, hands-on techniques in classrooms where they're encouraged by a caring adult and allowed to process the information they have learned with their peers" (1993).

This book, and particularly the stories which lie within, provide an opportunity for students to take ownership of their learning and as stated in the quotation above, learn science in a way that will give them a more positive attitude about science and to process their learning with their classmates and teachers. Used as intended, the stories will require group discussions, hands-on, minds-on techniques, and a caring adult.

The Stories

These stories are similar to mystery tales but purposely lack the final chapter where the clever sleuth finally solves the mystery and tells the readers not only "whodunit," but how she knew. Because of the design of the tales in this book, the students are challenged to become the sleuths and come up with likely "suspects" (the hypotheses or predictions) and carry out investigations (the experiments or investigations) to find out "whodunit" (the results). In other words, they write the final ending or perhaps multiple possible endings. They are placed in a situation where they develop, from the beginning, "the network of ideas in which to imbed activities," as Duckworth suggests (1986, p. 39). The students are also the designers of the activities and therefore have invested themselves in finding the outcomes that make sense to them. I want them to have solved the problem rather than having solved the teacher. I do want to reemphasize however, that we should all be aware that successful students do spend energy in solving their teachers.

In one story ("Seed Bargains"), twins Jimmy and Jeannine, shopping for seeds for a science project, are curious as to why two packages of beans are priced so differently. One package of bean seeds from the garden store is very expensive when compared to the package of seeds in the grocery store. The garden store salesperson says hers are better, but the twins are not convinced. Besides, what does "better" mean? The children intend to find out. The readers are challenged to help the twins find out as well, and thereby hangs the motivation. The problem, as perceived, must be put into a form which sparks the generation of hypotheses and the hypotheses must be tested through experiments—real experiments. Students are involved in developing problem statements and then in designing ways of finding answers. A common scenario following the discussion of this story finds the students running controlled experiments comparing the garden store seeds with the grocery seeds, inventing criteria such as percentage of germination, speed of germination, growing rate, mass of grown plants, amount of fruit, and so on. In the meantime they are finding from their activities and from other sources, the things they need to know about sowing seeds, nurturing plants, and creating the conditions for optimal growth. The biological concepts they learn are the direct result of their interest in and the carrying out of the investigation. Truly this is science as process and product. It also means that the students "own" the problem. This is what we mean by "hands-on, minds-on" science instruction. The teachers' belief in the ability of their students to own the questions and to carry out the experiments to reach conclusions is paramount to the process. Each story has suggestions as to how the teachers can move from story reading to the development of the problems, the development of the hypotheses, and eventually development of the experiments that will help their students reach their conclusions.

Learning science through inquiry is a primary principle in education today. You might well ask, "Instead of what?" Well, instead of learning science as an unchanging set of facts, ideas, and principles without any attention being paid to how these ideas and principles were developed. Obviously, we cannot expect our students to discover all of the current scientific models and concepts. We do, however, expect them to appreciate the processes through which the principles are attained and verified. We also want students to see that science includes more than just what happens in a classroom; that the everyday happenings of their lives are connected to science. Soaking seeds for planting, scraping frost off the windshield, or rolling objects down a ramp are only some of the examples of everyday life connected to science as a way of thinking and as a way of constructing new understandings about our world.

There are 15 stories in this book, each focused on a particular conceptual area, such as periodic motion, thermodynamics, temperature and energy, and sound and sound transmission. Each story can be photocopied and distributed to students to read and discuss in small groups or be read aloud to students and discussed by the entire class. During the discussion, it is the role of the teacher to help the students identify the problem or problems and then design ways to solve these problems.

Each story also includes a few "distracters," also known as common misconceptions or alternative conceptions. The distracters are usually placed in the stories as opinions voiced by the characters who discuss the problematic situation. For example, in "Moon Tricks," Frankie and his family discuss his puzzling observations of the Moon. Each family member voices a different possible solution to his questions and these opinions include many of the misconceptions we know to be prevalent in our population, shared by both children and adults. Where do these common misconceptions come from and how do they arise?

Development of Mental Models

Until recently, educational practice has operated under the impression that children and adults come to any new learning situation without the benefit of prior ideas connected to the new situation. But research shows that in almost every circumstance, learners have developed models in their minds to explain many of the everyday experiences they have encountered (Bransford, Brown, and Cocking 1999; Watson and Konicek 1990; Osborne and Fryberg 1985). Everyone notices the Moon and its phases; everyone has experience with differences in temperature as they place their hands on various objects; everyone has seen objects in motion and certainly have been in motion, either in a car, a plane, or bicycle; everyone has experienced forces in action, upon objects or upon themselves. Finally, everyone has been seduced into developing a satisfactory way to explain these experiences and to have developed a mental model, which explains these happenings to the satisfaction of that individual. It is also possible that individuals have read books or watched programs on TV and used these presented images and ideas to embellish their models. It is even more likely that they have been in classrooms where these ideas have been discussed by a teacher or by other students. In the film, *A Private Universe* (Schneps 1986), it was shown that almost all of the interviewed graduates and faculty of Harvard University showed some misunderstanding for either the reasons for the seasons, or for the reasons for the phases of the Moon. Many had taken high-level science courses either in high school or at the university.

According to the dominant and current learning theory called constructivism, all of life's experiences are integrated into the person's mind; they are accepted or rejected or even modified to fit existing models residing in that person's mind. Then, these models are used and tested for their usefulness in predicting outcomes experienced in the environment. If a model works, it is accepted as a plausible explanation; if not, it is modified until it does fit the situation. Regardless, these models are present in everyone's mind and brought to consciousness when new ideas are encountered. Rarely, they may be in tune with current scientific thinking but more often they are "common sense science," and not clearly consistent with current scientific beliefs.

One of the reasons for this is that scientific ideas are often counterintuitive to everyday thinking. For example, when you place your hand on a piece of metal in a room, it feels cool to your touch. When you place your hand on a piece of wood in the same room it feels warmer to the touch. Many people will deduce that the temperature of the metal is cooler than that of the wood. Yet, if the objects have been in the same room for any length of time, their temperatures will be equal. It turns out that when you place your hand on the metal, it conducts heat out of your hand quickly, thus giving the impression that it is cold. The wood does not conduct heat as rapidly as the metal and therefore "feels" warmer than the metal. In other words, our senses have fooled us into thinking that instead of everything in the room being at room temperature, the metal is cooler than everything else. Therefore our erroneous conclusion: Metal objects are always cooler than other objects in a room. Indeed, if you go from room to room and touch many objects, this idea is reinforced and becomes more and more resistant to change.

These ideas are called by many names: misconceptions, prior conceptions, children's thinking, or common sense ideas. They all have two things in common: They are usually firmly embedded in the mind and they are highly resistant to change. Finally, if allowed to remain unchallenged, they will dominate a student's thinking, for example, about heat transfer, to the point that the scientific explanation will be rejected completely regardless of the method by which it is presented.

Why Stories?

Stories are one of the most effective ways to get someone's attention. Stories have been used since the beginning of recorded history and probably long before that. Myths, epics, oral histories, ballads, and such have enabled humankind to pass on the culture of one generation to the next, and the next, *ad infinitum*.

Anyone who has witnessed story time in classrooms, libraries, or at bedtime knows the magic held in well-written, well-told tales. They have beginnings, middles, and ends.

These stories begin like many familiar tales do; in homes, in classrooms, with children interacting with each other or with arguing siblings, classmates and friends talking, or with parents or other adults in family situations. Sometimes the characters are animals in the backyard or forest that are given personalities and engage in discoveries and problem situations of their own. But here the resemblance ends between our stories and traditional ones.

Science stories normally have a theme or a scientific topic that unfolds, giving a myriad of facts, principles, and perhaps a set of illustrations or photographs, which try to explain to a child the current understanding about the given topic. For years science books have been written as reviews of what science has constructed to the present. These books have their place in education, even though children often get the impression from them that the information they have just read appeared magically as scientists went about their work and "discovered" the truths and facts depicted in those pages. But as Martin and Miller (1990) put it: "The scientist seeks more than isolated facts from nature. The scientist seeks a ***story*** [emphasis mine]. Inevitably the story is characterized by a mystery. Since the world does not yield its secrets easily, the scientist must be a careful and persistent observer."

As our tales unfold, discrepant events and unexpected results tickle the characters in the stories and prick their wonder centers, making them ask, "What's going on here?" Most important of all, our stories have endings which are different than most. They are the mysteries that Martin and Miller talk about. They end with a question, an invitation to explore and extend the story and to engage in inquiry.

Our stories do not come with built-in experts who eventually solve the problem and expound on the solution. There is no "Doctor Science" who sets everybody straight in short order. Moms, dads, sisters, brothers, and friends may offer opinionated suggestions ripe for consideration, or tests to be designed and carried out. It is the readers who are challenged to become the scientists and solve the problem.

references

American Association for the Advancement of Science (AAAS).1993. *Benchmarks for science literacy.* New York: Oxford University Press.

Bransford, J. D., A. L. Brown, and R. R. Cocking, eds. 1999. *How people learn.* Washington, DC: National Academy Press.

Duckworth, E. 1986. *Inventing density.* Grand Forks, ND: Center for Teaching and Learning, University of North Dakota.

Martin, K., and E. Miller. 1990. Storytelling and science. In *Toward a whole language classroom: Articles from language arts, 1986–1989*, ed. B. Kiefer. Urbana, IL: National Council of Teachers of English.

National Research Council (NRC). 2000, *Inquiry and national science education standards: A guide for teaching and learning.* Washington, DC: National Academy Press.

Osborne, R., and P. Fryberg. 1985, *Learning in science: The implications of children's science.* Auckland, New Zealand: Heinemann.

Research on learning. 1993. *Science Education* 77 (5): 497–541

Schneps, M. 1996. *The private universe project.* Harvard Smithsonian Center for Astrophysics.

Shapiro, B. 1994. *What children bring to light.* New York: Teachers College Press.

Watson, B., and R. Konicek. 1990. Teaching for conceptual change: Confronting children's experience. *Phi Delta Kappan* 71 (9): 680–684.

CHAPTER 2

USING THE BOOK AND THE STORIES

It is often difficult for overburdened teachers to develop lessons or activities that are compatible with the everyday life experiences of their students. A major premise of this book is that if students can see the real-life implications of science content, they will be motivated to carry out hands-on, minds-on science investigations and personally care about the results. Science educators have, for decades, emphasized the importance of science experiences for students that emphasize personal involvement in the learning process. I firmly believe that the use of open-ended stories that challenge students to engage in real experimentation about real science content can be a step toward this goal. Furthermore, I believe that students who see a purpose to their learning and experimentation are more likely to understand the concepts they are studying and I sincerely hope that the contents of this book will relieve the teacher from the exhausting work of designing inquiry lessons from scratch.

These stories feature children or animals in natural situations at home, on the playground, at parties, in school, or in the outdoors. Children should be able to identify with the story characters, to share their frustrations, concerns, and questions. The most important role for the adult is to help guide and facilitate investigations, to debrief activities with students, and to think about students' analyses of results and conclusions. The children often need help to go to the next level and to develop new questions and find ways of following these questions to a conclusion. The current philosophy of science education is based on the belief that children can and want to care enough about problems to make them their own. This should enhance and invigorate any curriculum. In short, students can begin to lead the curriculum and because of their personal interest in the questions that evolve from their activities, they will maintain interest for much longer than they would if they were following someone else's lead.

Interestingly enough, one of my students, a teacher, says that one of her biggest problems is to get her students to "care" about the topics they are studying. She says they go through the motions but without enthusiasm. Perhaps that same problem is not new to you. I hope that this book can help you to take a step toward solving that problem. It is difficult if not impossible to make each lesson personally relevant to every student. However, by focusing on everyday situations highlighting kids looking at everyday phenomena, I believe that we can come closer to reaching student interests.

I strongly suggest the use of complementary books as you go about planning for inquiry teaching. Three special books are: *Uncovering Student Ideas* (volumes 1 and 2), by Keeley, et al. published by the NSTA press and *Science Curriculum Topic Study* by Page Keeley published by Corwin Press and NSTA. *Science Curriculum Topic Study* focuses on finding the background necessary to plan a successful standards-based unit. Both volumes of *Uncovering Student Ideas* help you to find out what kinds of preconceptions your students bring to your class. I would also strongly recommend that you obtain one other book, *Science Matters: Achieving Scientific Literacy*, by Robert Hazen and James Trefil. This book will become your reference for all matters scientific. It is written in a simple, direct, and accurate manner and will give you the necessary background in the sciences when you need it.

One especially useful book is *Making Sense of Secondary Science: Research Into Children's Ideas*. The title of this book is misleading in the term "secondary science." In Great Britain, anything above primary level is referred to as secondary. It is a compilation of the research done on children's thinking about science and is a must have for teachers. David Ausubel in 1978 made one of the most simple but telling comments about teaching: "The most important single factor influencing learning is what the learner already knows; ascertain this, and teach him accordingly." I would also like to alert you to the September 2006 edition of the journal *Science and Children*, which has as its theme teaching investigation skills. In it are articles that will give you many ideas for teaching these skills.

On p. 11 is a chart showing the relationships among several of the various books mentioned above. Note that each story is matched with the appropriate topic in the *Curriculum Topic Study Guide* and the probe(s) in the *Uncovering Student Ideas* books.

The background material that accompanies each story is designed to help you to discover what your learners already know about your chosen topic and what to do with that knowledge as you plan. The above-mentioned books will supplement the materials in this book and deepen your understanding of teaching for inquiry.

How then, is this book set up to help you plan and teach inquiry based science lessons?

How This Book Is Organized

The stories are arranged in three sections. There are five stories related to the biological sciences, five for the Earth and space sciences, and five for the physical sciences. There is a concept matrix at the beginning of each section that can be used to select a story most related to your content need. Following this matrix you will find the stories and the background material in separate chapters.

Each chapter, starting with Chapter Four will have the same organizational format. First you will find the story followed by background material for using the story. The background material will contain the following sections:

Purpose

This section describes the concepts and/or general topic that the story attempts to address and where it fits into the general scheme of science concepts. It may also place the concepts within a conceptual scheme of a larger idea. For example, in "Moon Tricks," this section shows how the movement of the moon fits into a larger idea of periodic motion or motion that is cyclical and patterned.

Related Concepts

A concept is a word or combination of words that form a mental construct of an idea. Examples are *motion, reflection, rotation, heat transfer, acceleration*. Each story is designed to address a single concept but often the stories open the door to several concepts. You will find a list of possible related concepts in the teacher background material. You should also check the matrices of stories and related concepts.

Story in this book	Curriculum Topic Study Guide	Uncovering Student Ideas in Science		
		Volume 1	Volume 2	Volume 3
Moon Tricks	Earth, Moon, and Sun System	Going Through a Phase	Objects in the Sky	n/a
Where Are the Acorns?	Earth, Moon, and Sun System; Seasons	n/a	n/a	Me and My Shadow; Summer Talk
Master Gardener	Soil; Weathering and Erosion	Beach Sand Mountain Age	Is It a Rock #1	n/a
Frosty Morning	Weather and Climate; Heat and Temperature	n/a	Ice Cold Lemonade	Camping Trip
The Little Tent That Cried	The Water Cycle	Wet Jeans	n/a	Where Did the Water Come From?
About Me	Mechanism of Inheritance; Variation	n/a	Baby Mice	n/a
Oatmeal Bugs	Reproduction, Growth, and Development; Animal Life	Is It an Animal? Is It Living?	n/a	Does It Have a Life Cycle?
Dried Apples	Life Processes and Needs of Organisms; Cells	Is It Made of Cells?	n/a	Where Does It Go?
Seed Bargains	Plant Life, Experimental Design	Is It Living?	Needs of Seeds	Where Do Seeds Come From?
Trees From Helicopters	Plant Life; Reproduction, Growth, and Development; Adaptation	n/a	Needs of Seeds; Is It a Plant?	Where Do Seeds Come From?
The Magic Balloon	Density; Pressure and Buoyancy; Behavior and Characteristics of Gases	Is It Matter?	Floating High and Low	Why Is It Warmer?; Hot Air Balloon
Bocce, Anyone?	Forces; Motion	n/a	n/a	Falling Objects; Slippery Slope; Talking about Forces; Does It Need a Force?
Grandfather's Clock	Experimental Design; Variables; Motion	n/a	n/a	The Scientific Method
Neighborhood Telephone Service	Sound	Making Sound	n/a	Is It Scientific Inquiry?
How Cold Is Cold?	Heat and Temperature	n/a	Ice Cold Lemonade; Mixing Water	Ice Cubes in a Glass

Don't Be Surprised

In most cases, this section will include projections of what your students will most likely do and how they may respond to the story. The projections will be related to the content but will focus more on the development of their current understanding of the concept. It may even challenge you to prepare for teaching by doing some of the projected activities yourself, so that you are prepared for what your students will bring to class. For example, with "Moon Tricks" you may want to keep a moon journal yourself before asking your students to do so. In that way you will be prepared for the data they will bring to class and be aware of possible problems.

Content Background

This material will be a very succinct "short course" on the conceptual material that the story targets. It will not, of course, be a complete coverage but should give you enough information to feel comfortable in using the story and getting started on the inquiry. In most instances, references to books, articles, and internet connections will also help you in preparing yourself to teach the topic. It is important that you have a reasonable knowledge of the topic in order for you to lead the students through their inquiry. It is not necessary, however, for you to be an expert on the topic. Learning along with your students can help you to understand how their learning takes place and make you a member of the class team striving for understanding of natural phenomena.

Related Ideas From the National Science Education Standards (NRC) and Benchmarks for Science Literacy (AAAS)

These two documents are considered to be the National Standards upon which most of the local and state standards documents are based. For this reason, the concepts listed for the stories are almost certainly the ones listed to be taught in your local curriculum. It is possible that some of the stories are not mentioned specifically in the Standards but are clearly related. I suggest that you obtain a copy of *Curriculum Topic Study* by Page Keeley (NSTA Press), which will help you immensely with finding information about content, children's preconceptions, standards, and more resources. Even though it may not be mentioned specifically in each of the stories, you can assume that all of the stories will have connections to the Standards and Benchmarks in the area of Inquiry, Standard A.

Using the Story With Grades K–4 and 5–8

These stories have been tried with children of all ages. We have found that the concepts apply to all grade levels but at different levels of sophistication. Some of the characters in the stories have themes and characters that resonate better with one age group than another. However, the stories can be changed slightly to appeal to an older or younger group very simply. For example, in "Where are the acorns?" in Chapter Four, instead of a cute squirrel hiding acorns at the tips of tree shadows, you might find that a pirate (Jack Sparrow or one of his more naive shipmates of "Pirates of the Caribbean" perhaps) burying treasure while marking the spot with shadows would appeal more to older students. The theme is the same; just the characters and setting are modified. Please always read the suggestions for both grade levels.

As you may remember from the case study in the introduction, grade level is of little consequence in determining which stories are appropriate at which grade level. Both classes developed investigations appropriate to their developmental abilities. Second graders were satisfied to find out what happens to the length of a tree's shadow over a school year while the middle school class developed more sophisticated investigations involving length of day, direction of shadows over time, and the daily length of shadows over an entire year. The main point here is that by necessity some stories are written with characters more appealing to certain age groups than others. Once again, I encourage you to read both the K–4 and 5–8 sections in the "How to use these stories," because the ideas presented for either grade level may be suited to your particular students.

There is no highly technical apparatus to be bought. Readily available materials found in the kitchen, bathroom, or garage will usually suffice. You are provided with background information about the principles and concepts involved and a list of materials you might want to have available. These suggestions of ideas and materials are based upon experience while testing these stories with children. While classrooms, schools, and children differ, most childhood experiences and development result in similar reactions to explaining and developing questions about the tales. Whether they belong to Cheeks, the clever squirrel or Rani in her crying tent, the problems beg for solutions and, most importantly, create new questions to be explored by the young scientists.

Here you will find suggestions to help you to teach the lessons that will allow your students to become active inquirers, develop their investigations, and finally finish the story, which you may remember was left open for just this purpose. There is no step-by-step approach or set of lesson plans to accomplish this end. Obviously, you know your students, their abilities, their developmental levels, their learning abilities and disabilities better than anyone. You will find, however, some suggestions and some techniques that were found to work well in teaching for inquiry. You may use them as written or modify them to fit your particular situation. The main point is that you try to involve your students as deeply as possible in trying to solve the mysteries posed by the stories.

Related NSTA Press Books and NSTA Journal Articles

Here, you will find lists of specific books and articles from the constantly growing treasure trove of National Science Teachers Association (NSTA) resources for teachers. While the listings are not completely inclusive, you may access the entire scope of resources on the internet at *www.nsta.org*. Membership in NSTA will allow you to read all articles online.

References

References will be provided for the articles and research findings cited in the background section for each story.

Concept Matrices

At the beginning of each section: biology related stories, earth and space science stories, and physical science related stories, you will find a concept matrix, which indicates the concepts most related to each story. It can be used to select a story that matches your instructional needs.

Final Words

I was pleased find that Michael Padilla, past president of NSTA, asked the same questions as I did when I decided to write a book that focused on inquiry. In the May 2006 edition of *NSTA Reports*, Mr. Padilla in his "President's Message" commented, "To be competitive in the future, students must be able to think creatively, solve problems, reason and learn new, complex ideas…(Inquiry) is the ability to think like a scientist, to identify critical questions to study; to carry out complicated procedures, to eliminate all possibilities except the one under study; to discuss, share and argue with colleagues; and to adjust what you know based on that social interaction." Further, he asks, "Who asks the question?...Who designs the procedures?...Who decides which data to collect?...Who formulates explanations based upon the data?...Who communicates and justifies the results?...What kind of classroom climate allows students to wrestle with the difficult questions posed during a good inquiry?"

I believe that this book speaks to these questions and that the techniques proposed here are one way to answer the above questions with "the students do!" in the kind of science classroom this book envisions.

references

Ausubel, D., J. Novak, and H. Hanensian. 1978. *Educational psychology: A cognitive view.* New York: Holt, Rinehart, and Winston.

Driver, R., A. Squires, P. Rushworth, and V. Wood-Robinson. 1994. *Making sense of secondary science: Research into children's ideas.* London and New York: Routledge Falmer.

Hazen, R., and J. Trefil. 1991. *Science matters: Achieving scientific literacy.* New York: Anchor Books.

Keeley, P. 2005. *Science curriculum topic study: Bridging the gap between standards and practice.* Thousand Oaks, CA: Corwin Press.

Keeley, P., F. Eberle, and L. Farrin. 2005. *Uncovering student ideas in science: 25 formative assessment probes* (vol. 1). Arlington, VA: NSTA Press.

Keeley, P., F. Eberle, and J. Tugel, J. 2007. *Uncovering student ideas in science: 25 more formative assessment probes* (vol. 2). Arlington, VA: NSTA Press.

Padilla, M. 2006. *NSTA Reports* (May) National Science Teachers Association. *Science and Children.* 2006. Arlington, VA: NSTA Press. 44 (1).

CHAPTER 3

THE LINK BETWEEN SCIENCE, INQUIRY, AND LANGUAGE LITERACY

While heading into the final chapter before launching into the stories, I couldn't resist introducing you to a piece of literature that is seldom read except by English literature majors. The quotation that follows is from Irish novelist James Joyce in his classic book, *Ulysses*, written in 1922:

Where was the chap I saw in that picture somewhere? Ah, in the dead sea, floating on his back, reading a book with a parasol open. Couldn't sink if you tried: so thick with salt. Because the weight of the water, no, the weight of the body in the water is equal to the weight of the. Or is it the volume is equal to the weight? It's a law something like that. Vance in High school cracking his fingerjoints, teaching. The college curriculum. Cracking curriculum. What is weight really when you say weight? Thirtytwo feet per second, per second. Law of falling bodies: per second, per second. They all fall to the ground. The earth. It's the force of gravity of the earth is the weight. (p.73)

In his novel, Joyce's main character Bloom recalls a picture of someone floating in the Dead Sea, and tries to recall the science behind his fascination with the event. Have you or have you observed others who, while trying to explain something scientific, resorted to this recall of a mish-mash of scientific knowledge, half-remembered and garbled? (For this foray into literature, I am indebted to Michael J. Reiss who referred to this passage in an article of his in *School Science Review*.)

In his school days, Bloom seems to have been fascinated both with the curriculum and the teacher in his physics class. However, Bloom's memory of the science behind buoyancy runs the gamut from unrelated science language pouring out of his memory bank to visions of his teacher cracking his finger joints. Unfortunately, even today, this might well be the norm rather than the exception. This phenomenon is exactly what we are trying to avoid in our modern pedagogy and now leads us into the main point of this chapter.

There are many ways of connecting literacy and science. We shall look briefly at the research literature and find some ideas that will make the combination of literacy and science not only worthwhile but also essential for learning.

Literacy and Science

In pedagogical terms there are differences between science literacy and the curricular combination of science and literacy, but perhaps they have more in common than one might expect. Science literacy is the ability to understand scientific concepts so that they have a personal meaning in everyday life. In other words, a science literate population can use their knowledge of scientific principles in situations other than those in which they learned them. For example, I would consider people science literate if they were able to use their understanding of ecosystems and ecology to make informed decisions about saving wetlands in their community. This is of course what we would hope for in every aspect of our educational goals regardless of the subject matter. Literacy refers to the ability to read, write, speak, and make sense of text. Since most schools emphasize reading, writing, and mathematics, they often take priority over all other subjects in the school curriculum. How often have I heard teachers say that their major responsibility is reading and math and that there is no time for science? But there is no need for competition for the school day. I believe that this form of competition is caused by the lack of understanding of the synergy created by integration of subjects. In synergy, you get a combination of skills that surpasses the sum of the individual parts.

So what does all of this have to do with teaching science as inquiry? There is currently a strong effort to combine science and literacy, because a growing body of research stresses the importance of language in learning science. Recall, if you will, that hands-on science is nothing without its minds-on counterpart, since a food fight is a hands-on activity but one does not learn much through mere participation, except perhaps the finer points of the aerodynamic properties of Jell-O. The understanding of scientific principles is not embedded in the materials themselves or in the manipulation of these materials. Discussion, argumentation, discourse of all kinds, group consensus, and social interactions—all forms of communication are necessary for students to make meaning out of the activities in which they have engaged. And these require language in the form of writing, reading, and particularly speaking. They require that students think about their thinking and that they hear their own and others' thoughts and ideas spoken out loud and perhaps eventually see them in writing to make sense of what they have been doing and the results they have been getting in their activities. This is the often forgotten "minds-on" part of the "hands-on, minds-on" couplet. Consider the following:

> In schools, talk is sometimes valued and sometimes avoided, but—and this is surprising—talk is rarely taught. It is rare to hear teachers discuss their efforts to teach students to talk well. Yet talk, like reading and writing, is a major motor—I could even say the major motor—of intellectual development. (Calkins 2000, p.226)

For a detailed and very useful discussion of talk in the science classroom, I refer you to Jeffrey Winokur and Karen Worth's chapter, "Talk in the Science Classroom: Looking at What Students and Teachers Need to Know and Be Able to Do," in *Linking Science and Literacy in the K–8 Classroom* (2006).

The concept of linking inquiry-based science and literacy has a strong intellectual and research base. First, the theoretical work of Padilla and his colleagues suggests that inquiry science and reading share a set of intellectual processes (e.g. observing, classifying, inferring, predicting, and communicating), and that these processes are used whether the student is conducting scientific experiments or reading text (Padilla, Muth, and Padilla 1991). Helping children become aware of their thinking as they read and investigate with materials will help them to understand and practice more metacognition. You may have to model this for them by thinking out loud yourself as you view a phenomenon. Help them to understand why you spoke as you did and why it is important to think about your process of thinking. You may say something like, "I think that warm weather affects how fast seeds germinate. I think that I should design an investigation to see if I am right." Then later, "Did you notice how I made a prediction/hypothesis that I could test in an experiment?" Modeling your thinking can help your students see how and why the talk of science is used in certain situations. Science is about words and their meanings.

Postman made a very interesting statement about words and science. He said, "Biology is not plants and animals. It is language about plants and animals…. Astronomy is not planets and stars. It is a way of talking about planets and stars" (1979, p.165). To emphasize this point even further, I might add that science is a language, a language that specializes in talking about the world and being in that world we call science. It has a special vocabulary and organization and scientists use this vocabulary and organization when they talk about their work. Often, it is called "discourse" (Gee 2004). Children need to learn this discourse when they present their evidence, when they argue the fine points of their work, evaluate their own and others works, and refine their ideas for further study. Students do not come to you with this language in full bloom; in fact the seeds may not even have germinated. They attain it by doing science and being helped by knowledgeable adults who teach them about controlling variables or fair tests, about having evidence to back up their statements, and about using the processes of science in their attempts at what has been called "first hand inquiry" (Palincsar and Magnusson, 2001).

This is inquiry that involves the direct involvement with materials or in other more familiar words, the hands-on part of scientific investigation. The term "second hand investigations," refers to the use of textual, lecture, reading data, charts, graphs, or other types of instruction that do not feature direct contact with materials. Cervetti and Pearson put it so well:

> [W]e view firsthand investigations as the glue that binds together all of the linguistic activity around inquiry. The mantra we have developed for ourselves in helping students acquire conceptual knowledge and the discourse in which that knowledge is expressed (including particular vocabulary) is "read it, write it, talk it, do it!"— and in no particular order, or better yet, in every possible order. (2006, p. 238)

So you can see that it is also important that the students talk about their work, write about their work, read about what others have to say about the work they are doing (in books or via visual media), and take all possible opportunities to document their work in a way that is useful to them in looking back at what they have found out about their work.

Science Notebooks

Many science educators have lately touted science notebooks as an aid to students involving themselves more in the discourse of science (Campbell and Fulton 2003). Their use could also help English language learners (ELLs) develop language skills as well as understanding of science concepts and the nature of science.

Science notebooks differ from science journals and science logs because they are not merely for recording data (logs) or for demonstrating learning (journals) but are meant to be used continuously for recording investigations, designs, plans, thinking, vocabulary, and concerns or puzzlement. The science notebook is the recording of past, present, and future thoughts and are unique to each student. The teacher makes sure that the students have ample time to record events and to also ask for specific responses to such questions as "what still puzzles you about this activity?"

For specific ideas for using science notebooks and for information of the value of using the notebooks in science, see *Science Notebooks: Writing About Inquiry* by Brian Campbell and Lori Fulton (2003). In each chapter of this book, the teacher background material for each story will refer to uses of the notebooks.

I must acknowledge here the experience I gained in working with a teacher years ago in Pelham, Massachusetts, Dr. Marna Bunce-Crim. It was in her classroom that I learned the power of writing across the curriculum. In her classroom I witnessed minor miracles of children writing to learn and I came away with a great appreciation for the power of literacy in science education, especially the importance of asking children to write each day about something that still confused them. The results were remarkable, and as we read their notebooks we witnessed their metacognition, their solutions through their thinking "out loud" in their writing and in many cases, the solving of their confusions right there on paper.

The use of science notebooks should be an opportunity for the students to record their cognitive journey through their activities. In the case of the use with the stories in this book, it would include the specific question that the student is concerned with, the lists of ideas and statements generated by the class after the story is read, pictures or graphs of data collected by the student and by the class, and perhaps the final conclusions reached by the student and the class as they try to solve the mystery.

Let us imagine that your class has agreed on a conclusion for the story they have been using and that they have reached consensus on that conclusion. What options are open to you as a teacher for asking the students to finalize their work? It may be acceptable to have the students actually write the "ending" to the story or, alternatively, write up the conclusions in a standard lab report format. The former method, of course, is another way of actually connecting literacy and science. Many teachers prefer to have their students at least learn to write the "boiler plate" lab reports, just to be familiar with that method, while others are comfortable with having their students write more anecdotal kinds of reports. My experience is that when students write their conclusions in anecdotal form while referring to their data to support their conclusions, there is more convincing evidence that they have really understood the conceptual understanding they have been chasing rather than filling in the blanks in a form. Of course, it could be done both ways and two goals might be achieved.

As mentioned earlier, a major factor in designing these stories and follow-up activities is based upon one of the major tenets of a philosophy called Constructivism. That major tenet is that knowledge is constructed by individuals in order to make sense out of the world in which they live. If we believe this, then the knowledge that each individual brings to any situation or problem must be factored in to the way that person tries to solve that problem By the same token, it is important to realize that the identification of the problem and the way the problem is viewed are also factors determined by each individual. Therefore it is vital that the teacher encourages the students to bring into the open (orally and in writing) those ideas they already have about the situation being discussed. In bringing these preconceptions out of hiding, so to speak, all of the children and the teacher can address the alternative ideas about topics and analyze data openly without hidden agendas in children's minds.

The stories also point out that science is a social, cultural, and therefore human enterprise. The characters in our stories usually enlist others in their investigations, their discussions, and their questions. These people have opinions and hypotheses and are consulted, involved, or drawn into an active dialectic. Group work is encouraged, which in a classroom would suggest cooperative learning. At home, siblings and parents may become involved in the activities and engage in the dialectic as a family group. They engage in a lot of conversation.

The stories can also be read to the children. In this way children can gain more from the literature than if they had to read them by themselves. A child's listening vocabulary is usually greater than their reading vocabulary. Unfamiliar vocabulary can be deduced by the context in which it is found. New vocabulary words can be explained as the story is read. Teachers have found that children are always ready to discuss the stories during the reading and therefore become more involved as they take part in the reading. So much the better because getting involved is what this book is all about; getting involved in situations that beg for problem finding, problem solving, and construction of new ideas about science in everyday life.

Working With English Learner Populations

Suppose that part of your class is made up of students from other cultures and with limited knowledge of the English language. Of what use is inquiry science to such students and how can you use the discipline to increase both their language learning and their science skills and knowledge?

First of all, let's take a look at the problems associated with learning while having limited language understanding. Lee (2005), in his summary of research on ELL students and science learning, points to the fact that students who are not from the dominant society (e.g. western science) are not aware of the rules and norms of that dominant society. They may come from cultures in which questioning (especially of elders) is not encouraged and where inquiry is not encouraged. Obviously, to help these children cross over from the culture of home to the culture of school, the rules and norms of the new culture must be explained carefully and visibly and the students must be helped to take responsibility for their own learning. There are a number of books written about this topic, and I would not be able to cover the problem in this chapter as well as they have. You can find specific help in a recent NSTA publication entitled *Science for English Language Learners: K–12 classroom strategies*. Also very helpful is another NSTA publication, *Linking Science and Literacy in the K–8 Classroom*, specifically chapter 12, "English Language Development and the Science-Literacy Connection." Finally, an article from *Science and Children* entitled "Teaching Science to English-as-Second Language Learners" (Buck 2000) has many useful suggestions for working with ELL students.

I'll summarize a few ideas as best as I can and will also put them into the teacher background when appropriate:

- Experts agree that vocabulary building is very important for ELL students. You can focus on helping ELL students identify objects they will be working with in their native language and in English. These words can be entered in science notebooks and some teachers have been successful in using a teaching device called a "working word wall." This is an ongoing poster with graphics and words that are added to the poster as the unit progresses. When possible, real items are taped to the poster. This is visible for constant review, since if it is kept in a prominent location it is helpful for all students, not just the ELL students.

- Many teachers suggest that the group work afforded by inquiry teaching helps ELL students understand the process and the content. Pairing ELL students with English speaking students will facilitate learning since students are often more comfortable receiving help from peers than from the teacher. They are more likely to ask questions from peers than of the teacher. It is also likely that explanations from peers may be more helpful because fellow students explain things in language more suitable to that of their own age and development.

- Use the chalkboard or whiteboard more often. Connect visuals with vocabulary words. Remember that science depends upon the language of discourse. You might also consider inviting parents into the classroom so that they can witness what you are doing to help their children to learn English and science. Spend more time focusing on the process of inquiry so that the ELL students will begin to understand how they can take control over their own learning and problem solving. All students can benefit from being considered Science Language Learners (SLLs).

Helping Your Students as SLLs

How much help should you give to your students as they work through the problem? A good rule of thumb is that you can help them as much as you think necessary as long as the children are being challenged. In other words, the children should not be following your lead but their own leads. If some of these leads end up in dead ends, then a large part of scientific investigations is part of their experience too. Science is

full of experiences that are not productive. If children read most popular accounts of scientific discovery, they would get the impression that the scientist gets up in the morning, asks, "What will I discover today?" and then sets off on a clear, straight path to an elegant conclusion before suppertime rolls around. Nothing could be further from the truth. But, it is very important to note that a steady diet of frustration can squash a budding love of science. Dead ends can usually be looked upon as signaling a need for a new design or to ask the question in a different way. Most importantly, dead ends should not be looked upon as failures. They are more like opportunities to try again in a different way with a clean slate. The adult's role is to keep a balance so that motivation is maintained and interest continues to flourish. Sometimes this is more easily accomplished when kids work in groups. Scientists, too, work in teams and use each other's expertise in a group process.

Many people do not understand that the scientific process includes luck, personal idiosyncrasies, and feelings, as well as the so-called "scientific method." The most important aid you can provide your students is to help them maintain their confidence in their ability to problem solve. They can use metaphors, visualizations, drawings, or any method with which they are comfortable to develop new insights into the problem. Then they can set up their study in a way that reflects the scientific paradigm, including creating a simple question, controlling variables, and isolating the one variable they are testing.

You can also help them to keep their experimental designs simple and carefully controlled, and learn to keep good data records in their science notebooks. Most students don't readily see the need for this last point, even after they have been told. They don't see the need because the neophyte experimenter has not had much experience with collecting usable data. Until they realize that unreadable data or necessary data not recorded can cause problems, they see little use for them. Children don't see the need for keeping good shadow length records because they are not always sure what they are going to do with them in a week or a month from now. If they are helped to see the reasons for collecting data and that these data are going to be evidence of a change over time, then they will see the purpose of being able to go back and revisit the past in order to compare it to the present. In this way they can also see the reasons for keeping a log in the first place.

In experiences we have had with children, forcing them to use prescribed data collection worksheets has not helped them to understand the reasons for data collection at all and in some cases has actually caused more confusion or amounted to little more than busy work. On one occasion while circulating in a classroom where children were engaged in a worksheet-directed activity, an observer asked a student what she was doing. The student replied without hesitation, "Step Three." Our goal is to empower students engaged in inquiry to the point where they are involved in the activity at a level where all of the steps (including Step Three), are designed by the students themselves and for good reason—to answer their own questions in a logical, sequential, and meaningful manner. We believe it can be done, but it requires patience on the part of the adult facilitators and faith that the children have the mental skills to carry out such mental gymnastics, with a little help from their friends and mentors.

One last word about data collection: Over the years of being a scientist and working with scientists, one common element stands out. Scientists keep on their person a notebook, which is retrieved numerous times during the day to record interesting items. Memory is seen as an ephemeral thing, not to be trusted. Scientists' notebooks are treasured and essential parts of the scientific enterprise. They don't leave home without them.

And now, on to the stories, which I hope will inspire your students to become active inquirers and enjoy science as an everyday activity in their lives.

references

Buck, G. 2000. Teaching science to English-as-second language learners. *Science and Children* 38 (3): 38–41.

Calkins, L. 2000, *The Art of teaching reading.* Boston: Allyn and Bacon.

Campbell, B., and L. Fulton. 2003. *Science notebooks: Writing about inquiry.* Portsmouth, NH: Heinemann.

Cervetti, G., P. Pearson, M. Bravo, and J. Barber. 2006. Reading and writing in the service of inquiry-based science. In *Linking science and literacy in the K–8 classroom,* eds. R. Douglas, M. Klentschy, and K. Worth, 221–244. Arlington, VA: NSTA Press.

Fathman, A., and D. Crowther. 2006. *Science for English language learners: K–12 classroom strategies.* Arlington, VA: NSTA Press.

Gee, J. 2004. Language in the science classroom: Academic social languages as the heart of school-based literacy. In *Crossing borders in literacy and science instruction: Perspectives on theory and practice,* ed. E. W. Saul, 13–32. Newark, DE: International Reading Association.

Joyce, J. 1922. *Ulysses,* Harmondsworth, Middlesex: Penguin. Reprinted 1990. New York: Vintage. Page reference is to the 1990 edition.

Keeley, P., F. Eberle, and L. Farrin. 2005. *Uncovering student ideas in science: 25 formative assessment probes* (vol. 1). Arlington, VA: NSTA Press.

Keeley, P., F. Eberle, and J. Tugel. 2007. *Uncovering student ideas in science: 25 more formative assessment probes* (vol. 2). Arlington, VA: NSTA Press.

Padilla M., K. Muth, and R. Padilla. 1991. Science and reading: Many process skills in common? In *Science learning: Processes and applications,* eds. C. M. Santa and D. E. Alvermann, 14–19. Newark, DE: International Reading Association.

Palincsar, A., and S. Magnusson. 2001. The interplay of firsthand and text-based investigations to model and support the development of scientific knowledge and reasoning. In *Cognition and instruction: Twenty-five years of progress,* eds. S. Carver and D. Klahr, 151–194. Mahwah, NJ: Lawrence Erlbaum.

Postman, N. 1979. *Teaching as a conserving activity.* New York: Delacorte.

Reiss, M. 2002. Reforming school science education in the light of pupil views and the boundaries of science. *School Science Review* 84 (307).

Winnokur, J., and K. Worth. 2006. Talk in the science classroom: Looking at what students and teachers need to know and be able to do. In *Linking Science and Literacy in the K-8 Classroom,* eds. R. Douglas, M. Klentschy, and K. Worth, 43–58. Arlington, VA: NSTA Press.

THE STORIES AND BACKGROUND MATERIAL FOR TEACHERS

EARTH AND SPACE SCIENCES

Core Concepts	Moon Tricks	Where are the Acorns?	Stories Master Gardener	Frosty Morning	The Little Tent That Cried
States of Matter			X	X	X
Change of State			X	X	X
Physical Change			X	X	X
Melting			X	X	
Systems	X	X	X	X	X
Light	X	X			
Reflection	X	X		X	
Heat Energy			X	X	X
Temperature				X	X
Energy			X	X	X
Water Cycle				X	X
Rock Cycle			X		
Evaporation				X	X
Condensation				X	X
Weathering			X		
Erosion			X		
Deposition			X		
Rotation/Revolution	X	X			
Moon Phases	X				
Time	X	X			

MOON TRICKS

Frankie turned eight on April 2nd. For a birthday present, he got a new bicycle—a 16-speed trail bike so that he could go out on the trails with his mom, dad, and older sisters, Karen and Martha. But his best present was a room of his own. His parents had just bought a new house in the same neighborhood and the new house had more rooms. His new room had windows looking out over the backyard. His mom told him they faced east.

The first day in the new house was fun. All of the furniture from the old house had to be put into new places and it was like putting together a puzzle.

For their first meal in the new house, they sent out for pizza. Everybody was laughing and having a great time. But finally it was bedtime for Frankie. His mom and dad went up with him to his room to tuck him in. Frankie had placed his bed so that when he was lying in it, he could look across the room and out of some windows up near the ceiling. After he got into his pajamas, crawled into bed, and said goodnight to everyone, his parents turned out the light.

"Wow! Look at that!" said Frankie.

"Look at what?" mom asked as she stood in the dark room.

"The Moon! It's right there in the middle of my window! It's like a picture with a frame around it."

"So it is," said Dad. "Lucky you to have a room with the Moon looking in your window at bedtime each night."

The Moon was full—a big white circle, perfectly round and beaming light into Frankie's room. Frankie went to sleep easily. Even being in a strange room in a strange house seemed less scary since he had the Moon as his own night-light.

The next night, Frankie went up to bed and looked forward to seeing his new friend the Moon shining in his window. After the goodnights, the light was turned off and Frankie looked over at the window.

"Hey!" he shouted. "No Moon! Where is it?"

He bounded out of bed and looked up at the clear starry sky and saw no Moon at all. He felt cheated. The next night, no Moon again.

Two nights later, still no Moon at bedtime. What a disappointment! Bedtime wasn't as cool as it was on his first night.

A few days later, Frankie awoke in the middle of the night. A police car whizzed by the house, sirens screaming. Frankie sat up, frightened by the noise. He looked over and saw, to his amazement, his old friend the Moon, framed in the window. It was the Moon all right but it was not big and round. It looked like someone had cut off the right half of the circle.

Frankie was puzzled by this but too tired to think about it. It was 3 o'clock in the morning after all and he quickly dropped off to sleep again.

The next morning at breakfast he remembered what happened the night before and told everyone at the breakfast table what he had seen. Everyone seemed to have a different opinion.

Karen said there were clouds covering half of the Moon. She didn't know why it was outside his window at 3 o'clock. She also said Frankie might have been dreaming.

Martha thought that the Moon changed shapes through the night. She said it came up full and by the time it set, it was just a sliver of light.

Everyone laughed when Mom said she was pretty sure she sometimes saw the Moon in the daytime. But Dad agreed and said that maybe the Moon rose at different times each day. But that didn't explain the different shape.

Frankie was still left with a puzzle because nobody was sure of anything. Frankie wanted to be able to predict where the Moon would be at certain times and what shape it would have. How can you and Frankie find out why the Moon was showing up framed in his window at different times and in different shapes?

Background

Purpose

The apparent daily motion of the Moon and other celestial objects through the sky is a major science concept. This story is designed to call attention to the changes in position and shape of the Moon over time. It is part of a larger conceptual scheme known as periodic motion. Everything is in motion, and finding patterns that repeat themselves is one of the hallmarks of science. Other examples of periodic motion are pendulums, seasons, and sound frequencies.

The Moon is such a common object in the sky that it seems a paradox that the majority of the population so poorly understands this familiar object. It is probably the fact that it is so familiar that it is taken for granted, like the number of steps you descend as you leave your home each day or the color of your best friend's eyes. Therefore, the purpose of the story is to motivate students to observe the Moon each day, record their observations and find the patterns in the Moon's movement and shape. For older students, the reasons for these patterns might also be the curricular goal.

Related Concepts

- periodic motion
- time
- reflection
- revolution
- astronomical motion
- pattern seeking
- light
- rotation

Don't Be Surprised

Your students may well echo the comments given by the story's characters. Since you will be recording these ideas, they will constitute questions for your evolving curriculum. The most common misconception regarding Moon phases is that the shadow of the Earth causes the phases. Some students believe that planets other than the Earth cast shadows on the Moon. Clouds or other planets are often blamed for blotting out parts of the Moon and some believe like Frankie's sister that the Moon undergoes a complete phase change in one day. Research shows that these are common throughout the world and often persist into adulthood. Overcoming these ideas requires that students judge for themselves that the ideas listed above are not plausible, necessary, or not even observable. In order to combat the Earth shadow misconception, it is necessary for the students to experience a model that shows that the Earth does not enter into phase change and is responsible only for Moon eclipses. Most of these misconceptions are those voiced by some members of Frankie's family in the story. In this story Mom and Dad both made valid comments at breakfast.

Content Background

The first thing you will want to do is to keep a Moon journal yourself, as you might expect your students to do. You really should do this before you begin to teach this concept since it will prepare you for what your students will be bringing to class each day. (See the sections *Using the Story With Grades K–4* and *Using the Story With Grades 5–8* before you begin.) You will find that each day the Moon will appear to rise later than the day before. Since your students will be doing the same thing, you can expect the following data to be brought into your classroom each night the Moon can be seen, but of course you can expect that there will be gaps due to inclement weather.

If you began as suggested, on the night after the new Moon, you would find the Moon as a tiny, brilliantly lit crescent shape in the west, just before sunset. As the days pass, you would find that each day, the crescent would become more filled out until in about a week, it would be shaped like a half sphere with the curved side toward the setting sun. In the week that follows the "first quarter Moon," the Moon's lighted portion would continue to grow so that about two weeks after the first crescent appeared, the Moon would appear to rise in the east as a fully lighted sphere, the full Moon. By this time, you would also notice that the full Moon rises at almost the same time as the sun is setting. This observation would appear to suggest that the Moon and Sun would have to be on opposite sides of the Earth at this juncture. If the Earth's rotation causes the apparent rising and setting of the Sun and Moon, then the Sun's setting coinciding with the Moon's rising would best be explained by the Sun and Moon being at opposition with the Earth in the middle. Since the Moon's orbit is tilted slightly from the plane of the Earth's rotation, barring eclipses, the Sun would be shining directly on the Moon's surface showing all of it to observers on the Earth. Thus, a full Moon! This will appear as an important pattern since the Moon will have risen later each day. The major finding would be that you would have seen the Moon setting in the west just after sunset on day one of your observation and rising at sunset on approximately the 14th day or your observation.

By the night after the full Moon, the moonrise might be past your bedtime and that of your students. No Moon? The next day you see the Moon up there almost full in the daytime!! This may come as a surprise to many that the Moon can be seen in the daytime. As the time progresses to week three, the Moon is still visible in the daytime and very early in the morning and the curve of the lighted part of the Moon points in the direction of the sunrise! This is the Moon that Frankie saw at 3:00 am when awakened by the noises outside his window. By the end of week four, the Moon when visible is a crescent again but this time the curve is the opposite of what you saw on the first night. The next night you see no Moon at all, day or night and this is the "new Moon." Then the cycle starts all over again. It is important here to help the students realize that the light that falls on the Moon is reflected light from the sun and that the Moon does not have a light source of its own.

You and your students would also note that if you observed the Moon at a specific time each night, the Moon would appear a bit more toward the east in the sky as it is observed from your vantage point. It was observed further and further east until it finally rises in its "full" phase.

Your young students might well make a picture graph of their drawings and the shapes of the Moon over the period of time they observed. They can see the pattern of crescent to first quarter to full to third quarter to new to crescent again and so on. This satisfies the expectation of the early grade standards.

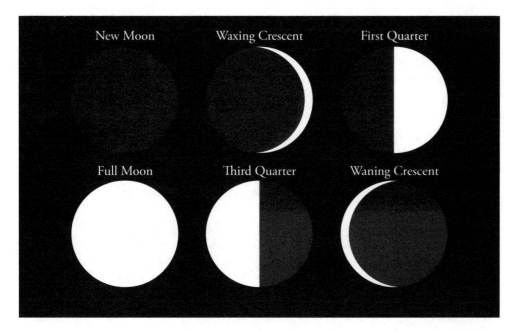

New Moon   Waxing Crescent   First Quarter

Full Moon   Third Quarter   Waning Crescent

If, as suggested in the "how to use the story" sections, you gave your students a probe or had them list the "things we know—our best thinking so far," on a large sheet of paper, the ideas that no longer hold water can be eliminated one by one as the evidence shows to the contrary.

The Moon revolves around the Earth approximately once every 28 days and appears to rise above the eastern horizon each day, moving across the sky to its setting point on the western horizon. Observers on Earth see this because the Earth rotates from west to east once each 24 hours and as the earth reaches the position where the Moon is visible in the east, the Moon is said to "rise." As the Earth continues to rotate, the Moon appears to move across the sky and finally to "set" or disappear below the horizon. In the meantime, the Moon also revolves around the Earth, in the same direction as the earth rotates on its axis, thus moving ahead, relatively speaking, of any 24-hour observation point on the rotating Earth. In other words, the observer sees the moonrise on day one, at a given time. At the next rising of the Moon, (day two) the Moon will have moved 1/28th of its revolution around the Earth during the elapsed 24 hours. Thus, the observer will have to wait until the Earth has moved a bit more than one revolution (24 hours) in order to catch up to the moonrise. This will result in a moonrise that will be a bit later each day. The average yearly difference is about 50 minutes per day but this varies from day to day and season to season.

Frankie was able to see the full Moon in his window by pure luck on his moving day. He expected to see it there night after night but this was not to be. First, the Moon rose later on the next night and on subsequent nights so that it was not visible at his bedtime. Second, due to the position of the Moon in relation to the Sun and the Earth, the Moon's lighted surface was visible from a different spatial vantage point from Earth and appeared to change shape from full to partial circle with its right half in darkness. This is referred to as the third quarter. Contrary to many beliefs, the Moon at this point is visible mostly during the a.m. from early predawn hours and the normal daylight hours to its setting before sunset. Then as the cycle progresses, a tiny crescent will be noticed in the western sky shortly before sunset and the cycle will repeat. Each day the Moon will rise later and more of the lighted surface visible from the Earth will become visible until the full Moon, which Frankie saw in his window. Then the lighted surface will begin to appear smaller until the new Moon, which is not visible since the lighted surface of the Moon is hidden from viewers on the Earth. So in summary, over an approximately 28-day period, the Moon's phases go from a new Moon, a crescent, a first quarter, full, third quarter, crescent, and back to new. (Actually, half of the Moon's surface is always illuminated by sunlight but due to our relative position to the Moon we may see only part of that illuminated surface.) Go to the following website for a demonstration: *www.noao.edu/education/phases/phases_demo.html*.

related ideas from national science education standards (NrC 1996)

K–4: Changes in the Earth and Sky
- Objects in the sky have patterns of movement. The observable shape of the Moon changes from day to day in a cycle that lasts about a month.

5–8: Earth in the Solar System
- Most objects in the Solar System are in regular and predictable motion. Those motions explain such phenomena as the day, the year, phases of the Moon, and eclipses.

related ideas from benchmarks for science literacy (aaas 1993)

K–2: The Universe
- The Moon looks a little different every day, but looks the same again about every four weeks.

6–8: The Earth
- The Moon's orbit around the earth once in about 28 days changes what part of the Moon is lighted by the Sun and how much of that part can be seen from the Earth—the phases of the Moon.

If you adhere to the National Standards and the Benchmarks in your curriculum development, you will want to consider the following:

(1) Grades K–4 children will want to focus on the **patterns** in the shape of the Moon changes from day to day. They can also look at the rising and setting times of the Moon for added information to solve the mystery.

(2) Grades 6–8 children will be guided into looking into the pattern and also into the **reasons** for the apparent changes in the shape and timing of the Moon cycle, thus gathering evidence for solving the mystery.

Using the Story With Grades K–4

Reading the story to the children, or having the children read the story themselves, is a matter of choice. A child's listening vocabulary is often greater than her reading vocabulary. Children enjoy being read a story and the reader can dramatize or emphasize certain parts of the story for effect. Since the story has no real ending, the children are asked to discuss the situation posed by the mystery. "What do we need to know in order to write an ending to this story?" There will be many ideas suggested, and we have found that the best way to use them is to record them on a large piece of paper, labeled, "Our Best Thinking Until Now." All ideas are accepted. Some may agree or disagree with various members of the family in the story, while others may suggest new ideas. When these ideas are posted, the reader, referring to the title of the page, suggests that each of these ideas or statements can be turned into a question. For example, a posted idea may be "Clouds cover the Moon and cause it to change shape." This can be changed to "Do we have any evidence that clouds cover the Moon and cause it to change shape?"

After this has been accomplished, the teacher asks the children how we can gather evidence to support or disprove the questions. The children usually respond by saying that they can "look it up" or with a little guidance, they can keep a Moon record for a month to see what they can find out. This leads to keeping a Moon journal in which the students identify a spot where they can observe the sky. The next question becomes, "What shall we record?" Here the leader can go back through the story and point out what kinds of things they have to observe in order to find the answer to the mystery. With guidance, the children will decide that the journal should include the time of the observation, the position of the Moon in the sky, how high it is in the sky and its shape. If the class can see the importance of keeping similar records, they can agree on a time (appropriate for their bedtime) and a method of recording so comparisons can be made when they share their journals.

Sending a letter home to parents explaining the project and asking them to help their child in remembering the time for observation and helping them to record all of the required data will give you some help. Students and parents will have to be made aware of the term *horizon* and its location even if mountains are present. It should be a point directly ahead of them where the sky meets the land. In mountainous regions, this would be at the end of the hand held out parallel to flat ground. The height of the Moon can be measured simply by using the "fist" method. Hold the fist of one hand, arm held parallel to the ground, at the horizon and then place the fist of the other hand directly upon the first fist. Holding that fist steady, move the other fist on that one and so on until the last fist covers the Moon. Count the number of fists and record this as data. Children of any one age group will have fists so close in size that little difference will be found among children to confuse the data.

The position of the Moon, as observed at the chosen time each day, will be important too, as it will move from west to east. We suggest that the students draw a landmark on their data sheet (a natural landmark or one placed on the horizon). Then students can mark the position of the Moon in relation to this landmark. It could be a tree, a house, a mound of earth, a bush, or a barrel. It is a point of reference since it never moves. Ask the children if it is important for them to observe from the same place each time. Discuss this with them.

Finally, the timing of the beginning of the data collection is of utmost importance.

It should be started the night or possibly on two nights following the **new** Moon. The reason for this is that the Moon will be visible before they go to bed. We suggest a time just after sunset in your location. During the autumn this should be approximately 7:00 p.m. Be sure to be aware of time changes due to Daylight Saving Time if this is prolonged to a later date. In order to know when sunsets and Moon settings and risings occur you will need a local almanac. *The Old Farmer's Almanac* is usually available at supermarkets or bookstores. There is usually one published for all areas of the country. Otherwise, many newspapers carry an almanac as well. You can also look on the internet for these times at *www. almanac.com*. This is extremely important because if you were to start this journal and data collection at full Moon time, the next risings of the Moon would become later and later and well past your students' bedtimes. With data collection beginning at first crescent, there are ample opportunities for viewing the Moon until its full phase. After that, until the new Moon, you can most often find the Moon during the daytime hours. Your almanac will help you with this.

Each day you can record the findings on a large chart so that the entire cycle can be seen. Weather may well interfere, with cloudy nights. If you can spare two months for observation this will usually provide enough data to complete a cycle. Obviously, you can carry out the Moon journal recording while engaged in another unit of study since it takes only a small part of the school day.

Finishing the story becomes apparent when enough data are collected that the children realize that the Moon rising later each night kept Frankie from having his "nightlight" each night. Had he gone to bed later each night, he might have had the pleasure of some moonlight but that is usually not the case. Since Frankie saw the 3rd quarter Moon a week later in the middle of the night, the later rising of the Moon and the phase change explains his observation. You can encourage the children to write the ending to the story as Frankie explains to his family what he has found that convinced him that the mystery is solved.

Using the Story With Grades 5–8

Most of the same techniques suggested for the K–4 classes are valid for grades 5–8 as well. However, the emphasis may shift to the reasons for the phases than on the presence of the patterns. Remember that many students, including college postgraduates, may be ignorant of the patterns and their ideas must at least be reviewed, preferably through a Moon journal. In the case of older students, they are usually developmentally ready to pursue the mechanics behind the reasons for the phases. It is important to go through the steps of discussing the Moon journal data so that the students have the opportunity to voice their preconceptions and test them against reality. Then the demonstration of Moon phases will have

much more meaning to them. Remember Duckworth's admonition that the student must have "done a major part of the work already, one has to have developed a network of ideas in which to imbed the [experiences]" (1986). Having discussed their findings and argued these data, the students will be more receptive to any demonstration. They may even have models of their own to try. This of course would be the best scenario but one must be prepared to provide a model for them to ponder if their models are not forthcoming or do not work.

Your older students are expected to explain this pattern and the obvious changes in the lighted parts of the Moon. As your students discuss their findings each day, they should be invited to manipulate three balls representing the Sun, Moon, and Earth in such a way that the observed Moon pattern (the reflected light patterns) could be reproduced. Having a floor lamp as a light source (Sun) might help or a bright light in the center of a darkened room would allow them to try different configurations of Sun, Moon, and Earth relationships. It will probably be noticed that in none of the configurations does the Earth's shadow need to fall on the Moon in order for them to witness a phase change. They might also notice that at the first quarter, there is no curve to the lighted portion, eliminating the misconception that it is the Earth's shadow that causes the phases. They will also see that it is impossible to create a gibbous Moon. They should have noticed that the clouds had nothing to do with the Moon's pattern from night to night and that the Moon does not go through the whole phase pattern eliminating other common conceptions.

Models for Explaining the Phases of the Moon as Seen From Earth

There are many articles devoted to this demonstration of the Earth-Sun-Moon relationship. It is important when using a physical model utilizing the children directly to try to be as true to the actual astronomical situation as possible. My favorite is one where students work in pairs, one being the Earth and the other moving the "Moon" which is a Styrofoam ball impaled on a dowel. A light with a bare bulb is placed in the center of a darkened room at about 2 meters above the floor with the student pairs arranged around it. The student in each pair who is Earth views the Moon from the peak of "mount nose," and spins slowly one complete turn, while the other student moves the Moon around the Earth each time the Earth rotates, in the same direction that Earth rotates. The Earth observer will notice that she has to turn a bit more than 180° in order to see the Moon because it has progressed in its revolution around the Earth. This will explain the reason for the later rise of the Moon each night, and the phase changes will also be obvious as the Earth continues to rotate and the Moon continues to revolve. Partners then switch and repeat the exercise.

It is very important that the students have the opportunity to struggle with their own models and observe the Moon firsthand before being introduced to the model described above. They should be able to see that this model allows them to verify the things they have observed and resolves the puzzles remaining from their prior attempts to create a model.

In addition you may read "The Sky's the Limit" from *Science and Children*, September 1999; "Look to the Moon," from *Science and Children*, November/December 1996; or "The Moon Project" from *Science and Children*, March 2006. NASA has a website which describes a Moon phase demonstration at *http://education.jpl.nasa.gov/educators/moonphase.html*. Additional resources on the Earth and Moon are available at *www.fourmilab.ch/earthview/vplanet.html*.

references

Driver, R., A. Squires, P. Rushworth, and V. Wood-Robinson. 1994. *Making sense of secondary science: Research into children's ideas.* New York: Routledge Falmer.

Duckworth, E. 1986. *Inventing density.* Grand Forks, ND: Center for Teaching and Learning, University of North Dakota.

Foster, G. 1996. Look to the moon. *Science and Children* 34 (3): 30–33.

Roberts, D. 1999. The sky's the limit. *Science and Children* 37 (1): 33–37.

Trundle, K. C., S. Willmore, and W. S. Smith. 2006. The moon project. *Science and Children* 43 (7): 52-55.

Yankee Publishing. *The old farmer's almanac,* published yearly since 1792. Dublin, NH: Author.

CHAPTER 5

WHERE ARE THE ACORNS?

Cheeks looked out from her nest of leaves, high in the oak tree above the Anderson family's backyard. It was early morning and the fog lay like a cotton quilt on the valley. Cheeks stretched her beautiful grey, furry body and looked about the nest. She felt the warm August morning air, fluffed up her big grey bushy tail and shook it. Cheeks was named by the Andersons since she always seemed to have her cheeks full of acorns as she wandered and scurried about the yard.

"I have work to do today!" she thought and imagined the fat acorns to be gathered and stored for the coming of the cold times.

Now the tough part for Cheeks was not gathering the fruits of the Oak trees. There were plenty of trees and more than enough acorns for all of the grey squirrels who lived about the yard. No, the problem was finding them later on when the air was cold and the white stuff might be covering the lawn. Cheeks had a very good smeller and could sometimes smell the acorns she had buried earlier. But not always. She needed a way to remember where she had dug the holes and buried the acorns. Cheeks also had a very small memory and the yard was very big. Remembering all of these holes she had dug was too much for her little brain.

The Sun had by now risen in the east and Cheeks scurried down the tree to begin gathering and eating. She also had to make herself fat so that she would be warm and not hungry on long cold days and nights when there might be little to eat.

"What to do... what to do?" she thought as she wiggled and waved her tail. Then she saw it! A dark patch on the lawn. It was where the Sun did not shine. It had a shape and two ends. One end started where the tree trunk met the ground. The other end was lying on the ground a little ways from the trunk. "I know," she thought. "I'll bury my acorn out here in the yard, at the end of the dark shape and in the cold times, I'll just come back here and dig it up!!! Brilliant Cheeks," she thought to herself and began to gather and dig.

On the next day she tried another dark shape and did the same thing. Then she ran about for weeks and gathered acorns to put in the ground. She was set for the cold times for sure!!

Months passed and the white stuff covered the ground and trees. Cheeks spent more time curled up in her home in the tree. Then one bright crisp morning, just as the Sun was lighting the sky, she looked down and saw the dark spots, brightly dark against the white ground. Suddenly she had a great appetite for a nice juicy acorn. "Oh yes," she thought. "It is time to get some of the those acorns I buried at the tip of the dark shapes."

She scampered down the tree and raced across the yard to the tip of the dark shape. As she ran, she tossed little clumps of white stuff into the air and they floated back onto the ground. "I'm so smart," she thought to herself. "I know just where the acorns are." She did seem to feel that she was a bit closer to the edge of the woods than she remembered but her memory was small and she ignored the feelings. Then she reached the end of the dark shape and began to dig and dig and dig!

And she dug and she dug and she dug! Nothing!! "Maybe I buried them a bit deeper," she thought, a bit out of breath. So she dug deeper and deeper and still, nothing. She tried digging at the tip of another of the dark shapes and again found nothing. "But I know I put them here," she cried. "Where could they be?" She was angry and confused. Did other squirrels dig them up? That was not fair. Did they just disappear? What about the dark shapes?

How can she find the acorns? Where in the world are they? Can you help her to find the place where she buried them? Please help, because she is getting very hungry!

BACKGROUND

Purpose

The main purpose of the "Cheeks" story is to get the children to learn something about the behavior of shadows cast by objects in sunlight. Although the story takes liberties with the "thoughts and projections" of Cheeks, one can take it as merely a motivational story. Some may be concerned with anthropomorphism but children read stories every day about animals that talk and have emotions. To leave these aspects out of the story would remove the "hook" that connects the students to the story characters. We believe that the teacher can make sure that children do not use these liberties to further misconceptions about the animals involved.

Primarily, the story addresses the motion of the Sun in the sky throughout the seasons, or what is called *daytime astronomy*. It is unfortunate that both of these conceptual areas are often relegated to students merely reading about the Sun's path through the sky during the seasons. Books and diagrams without the benefit of observation have become the main entryway for students to learn about Earth-Sun relationships. This is not necessary since measurable data about these motions are readily available to all students who live in places where the Sun shines fairly consistently.

Related Concepts

- rotation
- revolution
- Earth-Sun relationships
- measurement
- periodic motion
- axis
- seasons
- shadows
- time
- patterns

Don't Be Surprised

Your students may well feel that Cheeks is a victim of thievery if they have little experience with shadow lengths changing, either daily or seasonally. Others may have little understanding of shadows at all! It is not uncommon for students to believe that shadows bounce off objects rather than be caused by their blocking light. I have personally witnessed 7–10 year olds who had never played with shadows in any way. At the same time other students will immediately suspect the reason for Cheeks' error in judgement. Playing games such as shadow tag or messing about with shadows may prove useful.

A common misconception held by children and adults alike is that summer is warmer in the northern hemisphere because Earth is closer to the Sun. Actually, due to Earth's slightly elliptical orbit and most surprising to most people, Earth is further from the Sun during the time it is summer in the northern hemisphere. Another common belief is that the Sun is directly overhead at noon and there is no shadow cast at noon. Some students may also believe that shadows do not change in length at all, either daily or seasonally.

I cannot stress enough how important it is for you to collect some data by doing some shadow measurements yourself before trying this with your students. It will prepare you for the potential problems they may encounter and will give you some insight into what kinds of data they will bring into the classroom for analysis.

Content Background

The easiest way to begin is to find a place in your immediate area that is sunny most of the day. Place a dowel or pencil in the ground in the middle of a piece of paper that is attached to the ground by toothpicks so that the wind will not move it around. This stick is known as a Gnomen or shadow stick. (See Figure 1.) Make sure you put it in a level spot and then check the shadows cast by the gnomen every hour or so. You want to mark the shadow with a line that outlines the shadow. Mark the time as well as the outline of the shadow After a few hours, you will notice that the shadows cast by the gnomen move clockwise around the paper and as the day approaches midday, the shadow becomes shorter. It will be at it's shortest at midday, then begin to lengthen again. You will also notice that the Sun's apparent motion in the sky will correspond to the shadow cast in an opposite direction. In other words, the shadow will be pointing away from the Sun as it appears to move from east to west across the sky. This should give you a clue as to what to expect on a daily basis. You noticed that length and direction of the shadow change over the period of the day you observed. It should also have become apparent that as the Sun rose higher in the sky on its daily path, the shadow became shorter and that at the beginning of the day and after mid-day, the Sun moved lower in the sky and correspondently the shadow lengthened again (low Sun = long shadow, high Sun = short shadow). Your second observation should be that the shadow always pointed away from the Sun so that it moved from west to east as the Sun moved across the sky from east to west.

Figure 1. Gnomen

If you were able to do this for a whole school year, starting in the autumn, (and the following observations are correct only if you start in autumn) you would notice that the shadows would not fall in the same place on the paper from one day to the next. They would fall a bit further counterclockwise to previous shadows. Using what you found out about the relationship between the Sun and the direction of the shadow, you would surmise that the Sun had shifted its position at any given time a little to the southeast. In the northern hemisphere this would mean that as autumn proceeded and winter approached, the Sun would rise later each day and would rise a bit more to the southeast than the day before. The Sun is spending less time in the daytime sky until December 21st when winter officially arrives, also known as the "shortest day of the year." You should purchase a copy of the *Old Farmer's Almanac* at your local supermarket, bookstore, hardware store, or garden store. Specific tables give times for sunrises and sunsets for each day of the year. There are editions for each section of the country. If you do not have access to this book, the local newspapers also have an almanac which will provide you with astronomical times. You can also access the *Old Farmer's Almanac* online at *www.almanac.com*.

After December 21st, the "winter solstice," you will notice the opposite trend taking place. The Sun will be "rising" each day more toward the north and your shadows will correspondingly shift to this motion as you record them. The shadows will become shorter at any given time when compared to the shadows taken as winter approached. Your daily shadows will move even more to the south as summer approaches and the length of the day increases substantially. Unfortunately, school will probably end before the summer solstice on June 21st, when your midday shadow would measure the shortest of the year. Perhaps, if you are fortunate, you students will become interested enough to continue gathering data through the summer so that they can witness the entire cycle. From June 21st on, your shadow measurements will begin to lengthen again and the cycle will repeat as the next autumn and winter approaches. You would have had to make a one hour adjustment in your data collection for Daylight Saving Time in March. You would notice that on the day the clocks were changed to one hour ahead, the shadows you record would be an hour behind. You would therefore have to take your readings adjusted to Sun time rather than clock time. It is important to notice that Sun time is "real" time and that changing clocks does not alter the astronomical movement of the celestial bodies. I am reminded of the joke about the gardener who opposed daylight saving time because he thought that the extra hour of sunlight would be bad for his crops.

Your observations will eventually lead you to conclude, by means of your records of the motions of the Sun and the records of the corresponding shadows, that the Sun prescribes a predictable path in the sky and that each year this cycle continues. Further study may also lead you to the evidence that this motion is tied to the reasons for our northern and southern hemispheric seasons. This periodic motion is but one of many in the universe. In chapter 4 ("Moon Tricks"), you were introduced to the periodic motion of the Moon and its phase cycles. Each year you witness the periodical motion of the Earth and Sun, which causes the seasons, and each day, the rotation of the Earth to cause day and night. In chapter 16 ("Grandfather's Clock"), you will witness the periodic motion of the pendulum, which has a cycle so dependable that you can use it to keep time. It is no wonder that the big idea of periodic motion is so important as a unifying concept in science. It is also evident that science seeks patterns that eventually lead to predictions, which lead to a better understanding of our universe.

Each year the Earth makes one revolution around the Sun. In the northern and southern hemisphere a tilt of 23½ degrees accounts for the seasons. Since the

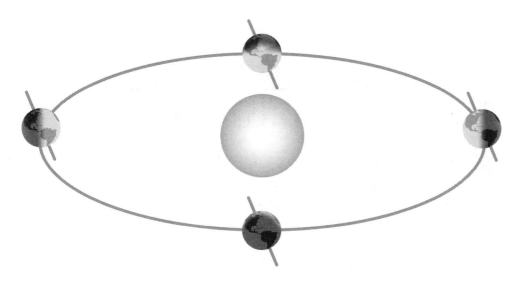

Earth's tilt always points in one direction, relative to the Earth's orbit there are times when the northern hemisphere is pointed more directly toward the Sun and therefore receives more heat from its direct rays.

This occurs at the summer solstice in June, the beginning of summer; days are long and nights are short. At the other extreme of its orbit, one half year later, the northern hemisphere is pointed away from the direct rays of the Sun at the winter solstice and days are short and nights are long. It is exactly the opposite in the southern hemisphere where the seasons come at opposite times of the year compared to the northern hemisphere. In between these two extremes, the Earth is in transition to either spring or fall and milder temperatures are common since the direct rays of the Sun fall more evenly above and below the equator. Days and nights are more equal in length. The tilt of the Earth is the main cause of seasons and of the differences in the Sun's position in the sky during the year and therefore

related ideas from National science education standards (NrC 1996)

K–4: Objects in the Sky

- The Sun, Moon, stars, clouds, birds, and airplanes all have properties, locations, and movements that can be observed.

K–4: Changes in the Earth and Sky

- Objects in the sky have patterns of movement. The Sun for example appears to move across the sky in the same way every day. But its path changes slowly over the seasons.

5–8: Earth in the Solar System

- Most objects in the solar system are in regular and predictable motion. Those motions explain such phenomena as the day, the year, phases of the moon, and eclipses.

related ideas from Benchmarks for science literacy (aaas 1993)

K–2: The Universe

- The Sun can be seen only in the daytime but the moon can be seen sometimes at night and sometimes during the day. The Sun, Moon, and stars all appear to move slowly across the sky.

3–5: The Earth

- Like all planets and stars, the Earth is approximately spherical in shape. The rotation of the Earth on its axis every 24 hours produces the day/night cycle. To people on Earth, this turning of the planet makes it seem as though the Sun, Moon, planets, and stars are orbiting the Earth once a day.

6–8: The Earth

- Because the Earth turns daily on an axis that is tilted relative to the plane of Earth's yearly orbit around the Sun, sunlight falls more intensely on different parts of Earth during the year.

Using the Story With Grades K–4 and Grades 5–8

- Please revisit the introduction to this book for the case studies about how two classroom teachers used this story. It will help you to see the overall picture of the process. Since the case study is available I will combine the grade level suggestions in one section. There are also a great many common elements for both levels, so to avoid repetition, please read ideas for both grade levels and choose the ideas most appropriate for your class.

the difference in shadow patterns. One helpful fact is that the further north or south of the equator you are, the greater the differences there are in day-night hour lengths and seasonal shadow lengths.

Cheeks, of course, fell victim to the misconception that shadows caused by the blockage of sunlight do not move or change shape during the course of the day or over the seasons. We have discovered that most children, from first grade on, immediately suspect that the shadow's position in the story had changed. The students do not often realize that the Sun's apparent motion is the cause of the changes in the shadow, although one or more students may suggest that this is the case. Students' experience is such that when pressed to explain something like Cheeks' problem, they begin to recall their simple knowledge of shadows and apply it to explain why the acorns were "lost." Once the older children have agreed that shadows do indeed change from day to day, they usually wonder in what ways they change and by how much. As seen in the case study in the introduction, younger children may be satisfied with focusing on what happens to the length of shadows during the course of a school year.

The story might raise some other hypotheses in the minds of the children about what happened to Cheeks' acorns. A few children may carry on with Cheeks' initial suspicion and make up ideas about thieving squirrels or chipmunks. This is a productive entrance to the literacy possibilities open to the teacher. These ideas can be encouraged by suggesting they write some creative narratives about Cheeks, who might be imagined to star in a multitude of adventures in the backyard. These are great entries in the science notebooks. Encourage the children to back up their stories with some facts they can uncover about the behavior of squirrels. This is an excellent door into the secondhand inquiry using textual or internet information mentioned in Chapter 3. For example, when children learn something about what a squirrel's nest looks like and how it is built, stories can emerge from or around these bits of knowledge. I have had children suggest that the acorns sprouted after they were hidden. This could lead into another investigation in the biological area about seeds to see if all acorns germinate immediately when planted. If the teacher feels comfortable in having two or more investigations going on at once, it can lead to an exciting set of concurrent experiments. These can be sideline excursions for some children even though the main thrust is aimed at the discoveries they will be making about the Sun's movement and the shadows which mark it.

With both older and younger children the facilitator should help the children realize that they need to explore what happens to shadows out of doors during the day. Older students are usually more interested in what happens to shadows over the seasons. With both student groups, it might be a good idea to let them play with flashlights and objects to study shadows and their relationship to light sources. Productive questions to ask might include the following:

(1) Can you make the shadow change its length? How did you do that?
(2) Can you make a shadow that is longer or shorter than the object? How do you do that?
(3) Can you make the shadow move around the table (desk) in different directions? How do you do that?

These kinds of observations also belong in their science notebooks along with questions that arise from their explorations.

Once they have had practice with making shadows, the ideas for Cheeks' problem may become more obvious to them. Younger children may come up with knowledge statements recorded on the "Our best thinking" sheet, such as the following:

- Outdoor shadows get longer as the day goes on.
- Outdoor shadows get shorter as the day goes on.
- Outdoor shadows change all the time during the day.
- Outdoor shadows point in different directions during the day.

Older students may have other misconceptions which they will share. These might include:

- At noontime there will be no shadow because the Sun is directly overhead.
- Noon time and midday occur at the same time.

As suggested previously, these knowledge statements can be changed to questions so the knowledge statements become productive questions, e.g. "Do outdoor shadows get longer as the day does on?" "Will there be a shadow at noontime?" These are obviously testable questions and can be changed back to hypotheses and tested. This may seem like an unnecessary step to go from statement to question back to statement but I believe it helps the children to see that hypotheses come from questions and that all knowledge should be open to question. It should also reveal that a hypothesis is a statement, not a question. Children should also be asked to give some reasons for their hypotheses. They need to learn that hypotheses are not merely wild guesses.

Once the children have given their opinion of why the acorns were missing, the adult can write these down on the "Our Best Thinking for Now" chart. I suggest that this list of theories or guesses about the motion of shadows be written on large pieces of paper and displayed in a public place. It should become a record of their "best thinking so far," and be modified as new ideas are incorporated into their thinking as a result of their activities. In this way they can revisit old ideas and see how they match with their new thinking. With new vocabulary, it is also a great help to ELL students. It helps them to remember where they have been as well as helping them see where they are going and that changing one's mind due to evidence is not a weakness. The hardest part of the adult role is helping the children learn how to look without telling them what to see.

The facilitator can help the children by asking some questions which can help the children focus on the problem and some solutions. Some of these questions for all students might be:

- What did Cheeks expect would happen to the shadows she used as markers?
- What do you think happens to the length and shape of shadows during one day?
- What can we do to find out what happens to the length and shape of shadows during one day?
- How can we make and keep records of what we find out?

For older students you might also ask:
- Do you think that the shadow Cheeks used changed in ways other than in length?
- Once the children have agreed on how they will study the shadows during a day and several days recordings are on display, the next question might be:
- How will we find out what happens to shadows over a longer period of time, such as fall to winter or winter to spring?

The next section on methods will discuss the use of the gnomen to collect data to answer these questions.

This last question and discussion of the data collection methodology will bring up many design problems which you must be prepared to address. The children will probably want to use a tree as a marker since Cheeks' dilemma is based on tree shadows. However, during the winter months when the Sun is low in the sky, tall trees can cast very long shadows which can be interrupted by the school building or areas of the school site which cannot be entered because of brambles or fences, thereby frustrating measurements. Explain to the students that since we do not know if or how these shadows can change, they might choose a shorter tree or object in the center of a wide space which will allow for all sorts of surprises without making data collecting difficult or impossible. One might be tempted to allow the students to find this out for themselves, but in the case of a study over a long period of time, this error can destroy not only the value of the data but the incentive to continue the study. Another way to prevent such disasters is to have several sites using teams of children at each site. If one site should run into problems, there are always data from the other sites. However, it is important that all teams agree on one method of collecting data so that any comparisons that might be required would be compatible. As a result of the discussion of the Cheeks story the children should be able to begin designing the data collection to answer their particular questions

One of the time honored methods for collecting shadow data is the gnomon. A gnomon is a stick which is placed in the ground or into a surface parallel to the ground with the stick perpendicular to the ground and which acts as an unchanging shadow producer. The stick blocks the Sun's rays and casts a shadow onto the ground in the shape of the stick. As the day progresses the shadow will change in two ways. It will become longer or shorter in length as the Sun gets higher or lower in the sky and it will point in different directions as the Sun moves across the sky from east to west. Depending upon the position of the Sun, the shadow may be shorter, the same as or longer than the stick. It is important that the surface upon which the shadows are cast is flat, not undulating or sloping. Of course, as long as shadows are measured at this exact spot each time, the shadows for each measurement will be comparable. If however, the placement of the gnomon is changed from time to time, as it probably will be, the level of the surface is very important. Paper can be placed on a board and the stick attached to the board at its center so that the shadows will be cast on the paper and can be recorded with pencil or felt-pen marker. You must only be careful that the place where the board is placed is level and not sloping.

If the gnomon is attached to a board, the board should be pointed in the same direction each time a recording is taken so the position changes can be noted. By this I mean that the sides of the board should be pointing in the same compass direction each time a reading is taken. If you want a really great class discussion, ask the students if it is important to align the board the same each day. The gnomon stick itself should be about the length of a toothpick so that the long winter shadows in higher latitudes do not go off the paper. You may want to add a triangle to the toothpick so that it looks like a pine tree and the story line is kept intact (see Figure 2).

Younger children can measure the shadow lengths with yarn or string and transfer the yarn to a paper to create a graph. Be sure to mark the dates and times carefully on the graph. You might want to have your children keep records of their measurements in their science notebooks. Children who are able to measure can transfer their measurements to a piece of centimeter graph paper and can compare lengths as well as directions of shadows. If these are placed on transparencies, shadow records from various dates and times can be superimposed on each other and compared for lengths and direction. It helps a great deal if each of the date's shadows are recorded in different colors so that comparisons can be made easier.

Figure 2. Tree Gnomen

Graph of shadow lengths, October to May

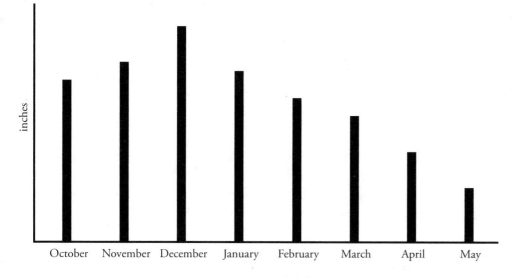

The children will find that there are several changes in shadows over short and long time intervals. These main observations can be listed as follows when considering shadows created by the sunlight. These concepts are:

- Shadows change daily and from day to day.
- Shadows always point away from the source of light.
- Shadows are longest in the early mornings and late afternoons.
- Shadows are shortest during the midday hours.
- The shadows change from longer to shorter and back to longer during one day.

Older students may add the following as well:

- Shadows point to the west in the morning and to the east in the afternoon.
- Contrary to expectations, in latitudes higher than 23.5 degrees north or south of the equator there is no time during the day when the Sun is so high that no shadow is cast.
- The shortest shadow is not always at noon. The shortest shadow is cast at midday, which is the midpoint between sunrise and sunset (often called local noon).
- Shadows at any given time change in length and direction as the year progresses.

All of these observations can help the students to understand the motion of the celestial bodies and ultimately the reasons for seasons. It is best to wait until middle school to expect any real understanding of the causes of the seasons. Their spatial relations will have developed by then and their ability to see the spatial relationships of the Sun and Earth will improve.

Related NSTA Books and Journal Articles

Bogan, D., and D. Wood. 1997. Simulating Sun, Moon, and Earth patterns. *Science Scope* (Oct): 46–47.

Driver, R., A. Squires, P. Rushworth, and V. Wood-Robinson. 1994. *Making sense of secondary science: Research into children's ideas.* London and New York: Routledge Falmer.

Keeley, P. 2005. *Science curriculum topic study: Bridging the gap between standards and practice.* Thousand Oaks, CA: Corwin Press.

Keeley, P., F. Eberle, and L. Farrin. 2005. *Uncovering student ideas in science: 25 formative assessment probes* (vol. 1). Arlington, VA: NSTA Press.

Keeley, P., F. Eberle, and J. Tugel. 2007. *Uncovering student ideas in science: 25 more formative assessment probes* (vol. 2). Arlington, VA: NSTA Press.

References

American Association for the Advancement of Science (AAAS). 1993. *Benchmarks for science literacy.* New York: Oxford University Press.

National Research Council (NRC). 1996. *National science education standards.* Washington, DC: National Academy Press.

CHAPTER 6
MASTER GARDENER

Eddie's mother was a professional gardener. She had a wonderful reputation in her business, Everything Green. People said she could make plants grow in the middle of the interstate highway. Of course this wasn't true but it showed how much people thought of her work. In fact she was out on a job the day the phone rang and Eddie answered it.

"Hi Eddie, I need to talk to Kerry about an errand," his Mom said.

Eddie handed the phone to Kerry. Sam's brother Kerry was 16 and could drive so he got lots of calls to help his Mom, especially during the planting season.

"Hi Kerry, I need you to do me a favor. I need you to take the truck and go to the farmer's supply store and get me two 80 lb. bags of coarse sand. That's coarse sand, the sand with big grains," she emphasized. "If they don't have coarse sand, go to the garden center and try there! I also need a big bale of peat moss. I'm over at Mrs. Brown's on Amity Street. Can you do that right away?"

"Sure Mom, be there in half an hour," said Kerry. He was a big shot since he could drive the pick-up and do things like that. As he was hanging up, he said to Eddie, "Hey little bro. Want to come along and see how the big folks work?"

Eddie ignored the little bro comment and said sure. He had nothing else to do anyway and thought that he might get Kerry to buy him an ice cream if he played his cards right.

Kerry got the coarse sand at the farmer's supply store and then headed for the garden center for the peat moss.

"Mom must have a real problem garden if she needs this stuff right away," said Kerry.

"What's a problem garden, anyway?" asked Eddie.

"She probably dug down and found lots of clay and needs to rebuild the soil."

"How can you rebuild soil? Soil is soil, isn't it?"

Kerry breathed a long sigh of impatience and told Sam that he should ask his mom when they got there. Eddie did just that.

"When I find a garden with too much clay in the ground, the water won't drain right so I have to rebuild the area by adding things that will break up the clay," his mother explained. "I add coarse sand to allow water to drain and then good rich soil and then peat moss to hold moisture and lighten the soil."

In the meantime, Kerry was lugging the sand and peat moss over to the garden where his mom was working. Mrs. Brown always composted her garbage and so there was plenty of good stuff in the compost bin.

Eddie's mom dug the clay up, broke it up with her shovel, added the sand, compost, and peat moss and mixed it up really well with her rake.

"There, now that should take this *Hydrangea* and make it happy," she panted.

On the way home, Eddie asked Kerry if he knew where all of this stuff, coarse sand, peat moss, and everything came from. "I thought dirt was dirt," Eddie said.

"Not sure, little bro. Better ask Mom. All I know is that I was told not to bring fine sand and I thought…'uh, sand is sand.' Must be different stuff on this old Earth that we don't know about. I thought sand was just…you know, little rocks. Maybe the different kinds of dirt come from different places. Maybe the sand washes up from the ocean in a different way to get to be coarse."

Eddie was puzzled. There was no ocean here. There are different kinds of sand? All soil is different? You can rebuild soil? If the answer to all of these questions were yes, then where did all of this different stuff come from and where would it finally end up? Isn't all sand alike? Isn't all soil alike? What is soil anyway and where does it come from? Now Eddie was really puzzled!

Background

Purpose

My grandmother, who was a farmer, often heard people talk about soil and call it dirt. Her response was, "Dirt is stuff where it doesn't belong. Soil is where we grow our crops." This story is designed to spur an inquiry activity about the process of weathering and soil formation. Evidence lies all around us if we look closely enough and ask the right questions. Eddie is helping us by asking some of these questions and we would like the children to ask some of their own questions as well. The result should be a better understanding of the materials that make up our planet and how they came to be.

Related Concepts

- rocks
- deposition weathering
- soil
- minerals
- erosion
- decomposition

Don't Be Surprised

Most students and a great many adults have the same questions that Eddie voices. "Isn't all soil alike?" "How can you *rebuild* soil?" The things we see everyday become so familiar that we no longer really "see" them or ask questions about them. I once visited a beach in Cornwall, England, sat down in the "sand" and began to allow it to filter idly through my fingers as I viewed the scenery around me. Imagine my surprise when I finally realized that a lot of this particular "sand" was made up of tiny shells of formerly living sea creatures as well as regular sand. I wondered how many people had visited that beach and never realized that they were basking on tiny seashells. When students actually begin to analyze sand and soil by looking closely at these substances with magnifying glasses or microscopes, their own questions will begin to form. We take soil for granted as we do sand. Sifting through soil samples from various locations will amaze children when they discover the many wonderful organic and inorganic materials that make up this common substance. There will be tiny bits of rocks and minerals, skeletons of once living creatures, minute living creatures, and as one little first grader exclaimed to me, "I found a bird's toenail!"

These observations will give rise to questions about how these little bits of rocks and minerals got to be so small, and that leads into the whole misunderstood area of weathering, erosion, decomposition, soil formation, and the importance of all of these processes in the Earth's past and future. Children and adults alike do not understand decomposition and the processes that return organic material to the soil. They believe that an apple that drops to the ground just disappears or miraculously becomes soil. Perhaps probing into the questions raised by this story will help raise their awareness of this common treasure.

Content Background

Rocks are made up of minerals. And what are minerals? Simply stated, mineral is a name given to substances that are not animal or vegetable. (Remember the question asked in the game 20 Questions "Is it animal, vegetable, or mineral?") Scientists believe that over the billions of years since the planet was formed, a process we now call the rock cycle has taken place countless numbers of times. Rock was originally formed by the volcanic actions so prevalent on the newborn planet that it was made entirely of molten lava. This lava contained all of the dissolved minerals we have in today's world. Over eons of time the Earth cooled, leaving us with a barren planet covered with this cooled lava which formed igneous rock. This is going on today in Hawaii, or Big Island as it is called. Volcanoes originally formed the Hawaiian Islands from deep below the ocean surface and these volcanoes, now above sea level, continue to spew out lava building more land and Big Island grows larger each day. In fact, deep within the sea to the southeast there is another island forming from an undersea volcano, which some centuries from now will become another new Hawaiian island when it reaches the ocean's surface.

When the Earth had cooled sufficiently to allow water to exist in liquid form, the seas and lakes formed and the water cycle (see the story in chapter 8, "The Little Tent That Cried") kept the Earth's water cycling from land to sky and back down again as rain. The volcanically formed mountains were broken down by weathering and water was able to run downhill to the seas, lakes, and rivers, carrying with it the broken pieces of the mountain in a process called erosion. Let's take a look at weathering and erosion and point out the differences between the two processes since they are often thought to be the same.

Weathering is a term that refers to the breakdown and changing of rocks and minerals. The processes causing weathering take place at the Earth's surface and are broken into three main types: chemical, physical, and biological.

When rocks undergo a chemical change, there are changes in many of the minerals in the rock. Acid in rainwater may come in contact with the minerals or rainwater may react with the minerals to form an acid. Some of the compounds and atoms in the mineral may actually go into solution in the water and be removed completely or the addition of oxygen may cause the mineral to flake off more easily. The higher the climactic temperature and the more moisture there is, the quicker the processes continue to work.

When mechanical weathering takes place, the rock is broken into pieces by actions such as scraping or grinding, repeated freezing and thawing resulting in expansion of water in cracks in the rock, and differential heating and cooling. All of these processes may cause wearing down of the surfaces or the flaking off of surfaces from the larger rock. Glaciers do their bit of grinding as well, thousands of years ago as well as today in places where glaciers still exist. Usually no chemical changes take place.

Biological weathering disintegrates rock and mineral particles due to the action of biological organisms. Examples include simple breaking down of rock particles by passing through an earthworm's digestive tract. Burrowing animals can exert pressure on rocks and bring them to the surface where they can be acted upon by other forces. Bacteria and fungi can cause chemical weathering by the chemicals they produce. Pressure exerted by growing roots can produce enormous forces. Perhaps you and your students have seen cement sidewalks pushed up or broken by tree roots. Plants can grow in cracks of rocks and cause the rocks to break up as the plant grows. And finally the carbon dioxide given off in cellular respiration mixed with water can lead to a chemical weathering by acid wearing away the surface of rocks and minerals.

All of these processes tend to weaken or break off parts of the larger rocks so that they can become prey to the process of erosion. As the rock particle is loosened or broken loose from the parent rock it can move. It usually moves downward due to gravity. Erosion is defined as the movement of rock or soil particles down a slope moved by some substance such as water, air, or ice and it may cause ruts or channels. If a particle is loosened from a rock and stays where it is, it is called weathering. Once the particle begins to move due to a flowing agent, it is erosion. The Grand Canyon was caused by both weathering and erosion. Chemical, physical, and biological processes of weathering loosened the particles of rocks so that the Colorado River could carry the particles off by erosion, cutting a canyon a mile deep into the surrounding rock.

These particles of the original rocks found their way into the seas and were eventually washed up on the distant beaches of the ancient seas. Most of the sand on the world's beaches is made up of quartz, the most common mineral on the face of the Earth. These formed layers of sediment (as sand), eventually were buried, baked and turned into sedimentary rock by combination of the heat and pressure of the land above them. This sandstone may have been weathered away again or it may have been buried and heated and squeezed further to form metamorphic rock. When life formed in the seas and the skeletons of the animals and plants formed layers of sediment, they became limestone and eventually marble if pressure was applied before it became exposed. As the earth continued its unrest and rose and fell, forming more mountains and in some cases lifting the newly formed rock to mountaintops the process began all over again. And on it goes to this day but we see only the results, because the process is exceedingly slow and cannot be seen even in many lifetimes. The process that produced the rocks, minerals, and soil we see today has been responsible for recycling the original material from Earth's origin and continues the cycle into the future.

However, we can see one process that is ongoing, namely the formation of soil and its continual enrichment. As the small particles of rocks and minerals are broken down further they are mixed with dead plant and animal material, broken down to their basic components by the action of decomposers like bacteria, fungi, lichens, and larger animals like earthworms and insects that live in what is now called soil. So in a metaphorical way, soil is a living organism, forever changing and recharging its nutrients so that plants and fungi can grow and gain mineral nourishment and replenish that which is used by growing, living things. Each time a once-living thing enters the soil it is broken down into its most basic components by decomposers and keeps the soil rich and fertile. Eddie's mother refers to the fact that her client composts and therefore has good soil that she can use. Her client composts by putting only the vegetable matter from her garbage into a container along with water, soil, and the organisms that break down the vegetable matter. The person who composts is feeding the organisms in the soil so they can break down the vegetable material into nutrients that can be used by plants. Remember, these nutrients are not food but include elements such as copper, magnesium, potassium, and phosphorus, as well as nitrogen and calcium that are necessary for plants to function. Gardeners often add fertilizers containing these necessary nutrients to the soil. These are erroneously called "plant food," but are more like the vitamins and minerals we take to supplement our own food intake. Since plants are producers, they make their own food, so speaking of fertilizers as plant food is incorrect and confusing.

Soil can be one of three main types: sandy, silty, or clay. Besides the living things in the soil there are rock and mineral particles that differ in size and structure. Sandy soil is composed of larger particles with lots of space between them, which allow great drainage but retain little water and dissolved minerals. Silty soil is made up of much smaller particles visible only by microscope and is formed by mechanical weathering. It is often seen as dust and can be blown by wind for miles.

Clay is formed mainly by chemical weathering and is made up of tiny closely packed particles visible only through an electron microscope. It has poor drainage and is structured in layers that make it difficult for plants to penetrate.

Soil has texture and structure. The texture of the soil is determined by the proportions of sand, silt, and clay and by which one dominates the properties of the soil. You cannot easily change the texture of the soil but you can change the structure of the soil, which is the arrangement of the different types of soil it contains. Eddie's mom changed the structure of the soil, dominated by the clay texture, by adding organic material such as peat moss to hold water, compost to add nutrients, and sand to improve drainage. Good growing soil is loose and crumbly and takes in water easily, allows air to move in and out, and allows for plant roots to penetrate easily finding the water and nutrients they need. Good growing soil does not form thick, heavy clods. Eddie's mom did just this as she rebuilt the soil structure.

related Ideas From National Science education standards (NrC 1996)

K–4: Changes in the Earth and Sky
- The surface of the Earth changes. Some changes are due to slow processes, such as weathering and erosion.

K–4: Properties of Earth Materials
- Earth materials are solid rocks and soils, water and gases of the atmosphere. The varied materials have different physical and chemical properties, which make them useful in different ways, for example, as building materials, as sources of fuel, or for growing the plants we use as food. Earth materials provide many of the resources that humans use.
- Soils have properties of color and texture, capacity to retain water and

ability to support the growth of many kinds of plants, including those in our food supply.

5–8: Structure of the Earth System

- Soil consists of weathered rocks and decomposed organic material from dead plants and animals and bacteria. Soils are often found in layers with each having a different chemical composition and texture.
- Landforms are the result of a combination of constructive and destructive forces. Constructive forces include crystal deformation, volcanic eruption, and deposition of sediment, while destructive forces include weathering and erosion.
- Some changes in the solid earth can be described as the "rock cycle." Old rocks at the Earth's surface weather, forming sediments that are buried, then compacted, heated, and often recrystallized into rock.

related ideas from Benchmarks for Science Literacy (aaas 1993)

K–2: Processes That Shape the Earth

- Chunks of rock come in many sizes and shapes, from boulders to grains of sand and even smaller.

3–5: Processes That Shape the Earth

- Waves, wind, water, and ice shape and reshape the Earth's land surface by eroding rock and soil in some areas and depositing them in other areas, sometimes in seasonal layers.
- Rock is composed of different combinations of minerals. Smaller rocks come from the breakage and weathering of bedrock and larger rocks. Soil is made partly from weathered rock, partly from plant remains—and also contains many living organisms.

6–8: Processes That Shape the Earth

- Although weathered rock is the basic component of soil, the composition and texture of soil and its fertility and resistance to erosion are greatly influenced by plant roots and debris, bacteria, fungi, worms, insects, rodents, and other organisms.
- Some changes in the Earth's surface are abrupt (such as earthquakes and volcanic eruptions) while other changes happen very slowly (such as uplift and wearing down of mountains). The Earth's surface is shaped in part by the motion of water and wind over very long times, which acts to level mountain ranges.

Using the Story With Grades K–4

I would like to suggest that you consider using the probe, "Beach Sand," in the book *Uncovering Student Ideas in Science, Volume 1* (Keeley, Eberle, and Farrin 2005) even before reading this chapter's story to your students. You will learn what kinds of preconceptions your students are bringing to your class and which ones will have to be addressed.

One of the biggest problems in studying this topic with young children is the time scale involved. How many of us can really comprehend a million of anything, much less a billion? The wearing down of mountains must seem like an impossible fairy tale to a young child but they can observe the particles of rocks and minerals in common objects like soil and sand. After reading the story, children are often anxious to take a look at different types of sand and soil. If you have different gauges of strainers, the children can separate the different sizes of sand by sifting them. But one of the most effective ways of beginning with young children is to let them use magnifiers and toothpicks to work their way through a small amount of soil taken from the garden or the school property. They may need to have help learning how to use the magnifiers or you may use the type held on tripod stands. Using a magnifier involves holding the glass up to the eye and bringing the object to be observed up to the eye rather than putting the magnifier down near the object. My experience is that children will enjoy finding things in the soil and trying to identify them. Of course these should be recorded in their science notebooks with plenty of labeled drawings. The analysis of soil should reveal that it is made up of many different things, including living and once living material, and nonliving material such as water and tiny particles of rocks and minerals.

Using the same techniques with a small helping of sand is also rewarding and asking the children to sort, with the aid of a magnifier, the different types of grains in piles that "go together" will show them that sand is a mixture of many beautiful and newly discovered little rocks and minerals of amazing varieties of size, shape, color, and luster. If possible, try to obtain sand samples from several different locations. Even though quartz will usually be the dominant mineral, sand from different locations can be sharp or rounded or fragmented. If you get coral sand or green or black sand the differences will be dramatic. There may even be a few little seashells. Comparing these grains to larger rocks that contain the same kinds of minerals and crystals will usually convince students of the origin of the sand. During discussions, students are made aware of the continuity between the small grains and the larger rocks and boulders they may see in the naturally visible world. A ten-minute field trip to find rocks and minerals in the natural world is well worthwhile and broadens their understanding of the connections to larger landforms. And in this connection you may help them to see that the wearing down of boulders into sand will take a long, long time. For young children this is a first step toward understanding the time scale involved.

Third and fourth graders can also benefit from some of the same kinds of activities as described above. One can expect a bit more sophistication in their recording and drawings of what they find. They can also learn to categorize these rocks by color, luster, and hardness and some students may benefit from learning the differences between igneous, sedimentary, and metamorphic rocks. There are many commercial units on rocks and minerals for follow-up work but the inquiry

they do on sand and soil will prepare them better for working with these programs of identification and categorization of rocks and minerals in later grades.

I might suggest that you consider planting seeds in different kinds of soils, keeping all other variables constant to see if there are differences in germination ratios, germination time, health of plants, and size of plants, etc. Older students might also use kits that determine the amount of various minerals in types of soils that affect plant growth.

Using the Story With Grades 5–8

I would again suggest that you consider giving your students the probe "Beach Sand," found in *Uncovering Student Ideas in Science, Volume 1* (Keeley, Eberle, and Farrin 2005). You may also want to use the probe "Mountain Age," in the same book. These probes will provide you with knowledge of the preconceptions your students bring to class on the topic of the rock cycle.

Upper elementary-level and middle school students may have already done some study of weathering in earlier grades. The probe will give you an idea of how many of their preconceptions were changed by past instruction. Their conception of long periods of time will probably be more mature but they will need to explore the questions Eddie has about the origin of rocks, sand, and soil by developing questions of their own. Mark Girod, in his article "Sublime Science," in the February 2007 issue of *Science and Children* gives some wonderful suggestions on how to help children understand the magnitude of large numbers. By using pages printed with 10,000 dots (done on the computer) he was able to show his students large numbers, and through a series of activities involving counting and the guessing of numbers the students were able to actually see what large numbers of objects looked like. Imagine, 10 sheets of 10,000 dots actually showed students what a million looked like.

After reading the story, you may want to develop a chart of their "best thinking" for periodic review as they go about their inquiry. The gardening theme of the story is aimed at making them wonder about the various types of materials on the Earth. If you are fortunate, you may already have a "rock hound" or two in your class. If this is the case, you may have direct access to a lapidary rock tumbler. This small device, which is usually used to wear down and polish rocks and minerals into beautiful stones, can also be used to show in quick time the process of weathering that takes centuries in the real world. Your local Earth science teacher may have a tumbler you can borrow. They are quite inexpensive and can be usually found in local craft stores.

Your students' inquiry questions may have more to do with comparing different kinds of sand from various locations or comparing different types of soil or even doing a survey of biomass (available natural food, like insects or plant matter) in various soils, than they do on the age of the Earth.

One must always be aware of the possibility of children coming from homes where biblical stories are considered to be literal truth. These children will believe that the Earth is only 6,000 years old and base their beliefs on faith alone. While we, as teachers, cannot argue science versus faith questions, we can state specifically that the numbers science considers to be true are based upon scientific tests and verified theories. There is no use arguing science and religion in a science classroom since they are based on two entirely different systems of belief and verification. This may also give you an opportunity to discuss the nature of science with your students if this seems appropriate.

You may also consider using a stream table, which allows the students to simulate, in quick time, the erosion and deposition of soil or sand by running water. Plans for simple stream tables can be found easily on the internet. Care must be taken to emphasize that the erosion sometimes seen in a stream table may take much longer to accomplish in the real world. They should be aware that natural disasters like tsunamis, hurricanes, and tornadoes might change the landscape very quickly but that the normal cutting of canyons and valleys and the creation of such landforms as the Devils Tower take thousands if not millions of years. The stream table is only a model used to test out theories to see if they can prove to be true in a longer time frame.

Thinking and learning about the enormous time frame for the building and rebuilding of Earth's landforms may seem to be a daunting task but it is a particularly important concept for students to master, especially since we are capable of modifying so many parts of Earth through our negligence and hurry to change the planet for our own benefit and greed. One can never go wrong in teaching our children about their responsibility as stewards of our natural resources.

RELATED NSTA BOOKS AND JOURNAL ARTICLES

Coffey, P., and S. Mattox. 2006. Take a tumble. *Science and Children* 43 (7): 33–37.

Driver, R., A. Squires, P. Rushworth, and V. Wood-Robinson. 1994. *Making sense of secondary science: Research into children's ideas.* London and New York: Routledge Falmer.

Gibb, L. 2000. Second grade soil scientists. *Science and Children* 38 (3): 24–28.

Girod, M. 2007. Sublime science. *Science and Children* 44 (6): 26–29.

Keeley, P. 2005. *Science curriculum topic study: Bridging the gap between standards and practice.* Thousand Oaks, CA: Corwin Press.

Keeley, P., F. Eberle, and L. Farrin. 2005. *Uncovering student ideas in science: 25 formative assessment probes* (vol. 1). Arlington, VA: NSTA Press.

Keeley, P., F. Eberle, and J. Tugel. 2007. *Uncovering student ideas in science: 25 more formative assessment probes* (vol. 2). Arlington, VA: NSTA Press.

Laroder, A., D. Tippins, V. Handa, and L. Morano. 2007. Rock showdown. *Science Scope* 30 (7): 32–37.

Levine, I. 2000. The crosswicks rock caper. *Science and Children* 37 (4): 26–29.

McDuffy, T. 2003. Sand, up close and amazing. *Science Scope* 27 (1): 31–35.

Sexton, U. 1997. Science learning in the sand. *Science and Children* 34 (4): 28–31; 40–42.

Verilar, M., and T. B. Benhart. 2004. Welcome to rock day. *Science and Children* 41 (4): 40–45.

REFERENCES

Gibb, L. 2000. Second grade soil scientists. *Science and Children* 38 (3) 24-28.

Keeley, P., F. Eberle, and L. Farrin. 2005. *Uncovering student ideas in science: 25 formative assessment probes* (vol. 1). Arlington, VA: NSTA Press.

CHAPTER 7

FROSTY MORNING

Andy turned his 8-year-old body over in his bed as the first rays of daylight peeked into his bedroom window. It looked like another cold morning. He could tell because the birds huddled around the feeder were all fluffed up and looked like they were wearing down vests under their feathers. The bird feeder was hanging from a tree just outside his window and the blowing wind made the feeder sway as though the birds were using it as a swing.

"Cold out there," thought Andy, "and the wind will make it feel colder! Wind does that."

Katie, Andy's older sister who was nine, awoke on the other side of the house in her bed next to a window, which in winter framed the rising Sun. The golden windowpane seemed to brighten her spirits and the warm glow of the Sun made the room feel cozy. "Beautiful day," Katie said to herself. "We'll be able to have outside gym today."

At breakfast, Katie and Andy sat at the table eating their cereal and saying very little. Both children started slowly in the morning and needed a bit of time to get their minds and bodies moving. In fact, everyone was slow this morning. Mom had overslept, the children had dawdled, and the school bus had honked and gone before they could get out of the front door and down the driveway.

"Mom," whined Andy, "we missed the bus. Now what? Do we stay home today?"

"No way!" shouted Katie. "I'm in an assembly play today. I can't miss school."

"I guess I'll have to drive you," said Mother sadly. She had hoped to get in an extra hour's sleep after the children had left since she had been up late the night before. "But, you'll have to help. While I get dressed you two run out and scrape the frost off the car windows, front and back. Katie, you take the back windows and Andy the front. And do a good job!"

The children got the scrapers out of the car trunk and went about their work. The car was parked in the front driveway but it was pulled into a little "L" shaped carport so that the front end was surrounded on two sides by the house and the woodshed. The rear of the car stuck right out into the drive. Andy squeezed through the space between the house and the front fender and prepared to scrape. He could hear the sounds of Katie's scraper as it sliced through the white icing on the rear window.

"Wait a minute," he thought. The windshield was completely clear. "This is cool," he thought with a smile. "Katie is still scraping and my glass is clear as can be. Maybe I won't tell her." But he couldn't resist grinning when Katie came forward and saw that the windshield and front side windows were clear and dry.

She figured it out in a flash. "No fair!' she shouted. "You didn't have to do anything."

"That's right," laughed Andy. "Hope you didn't wear yourself out back there. Mom's going to love the way my windows are clear and shiny. Yours have a lot of streaks on them. Better go back and do a good job."

Just at that moment when Katie was going to demand that Andy go back and finish up on the rear windows, Mom came out of the house and began shooing them into car. "Let's go or you'll be really late."

"Nice job on the windows kids," she said. "The windshield is especially clear Andy. How did you do that?"

"It was easy," said Andy feeling Kate's angry eyes boring into the back of his head.

"He didn't do anything," cried Katie. "His windows didn't have any frost on them at all."

"How could that be?" asked Mom. "One end of the car was frosted and the other one wasn't?"

"Must have been the Sun," said Andy smugly.

"The car was parked completely in the shadows," Katie offered.

"Well then, the front end of the car was warmer than the back end," replied Andy.

"Why?" asked Mom. "I always thought that the air around the house was the same no matter where is was located. Didn't you?"

"The front end of the car was really close to the house," said Katie. "Could that have anything to do with it?"

"Would that make the temperature there different than any other place around

the yard?" asked Andy. "Are there places in our yard or around our house that have different temperatures?"

"I guess there are ways to find out," said Mother. "But right now, we need to get you guys to school."

Background

Purpose

The theme of the story can be summed up in one word: microclimates. Have you noticed that there are variations among the temperatures broadcasted on your radio or TV and your own thermometer? Have you noticed that there are differences in temperature depending upon where you place your thermometer? Have you noticed that certain plants do better or worse depending upon where in your yard they are planted? This story highlights the fact that there are physical differences in every location that modify the amount of heat that is distributed in and around that location. This creates little islands of climatic diversity called microclimates. This story should result in deeper understanding of the effects of differential heating of the Earth's surface by the Sun.

Related Concepts

- atmosphere
- solar energy
- heat
- melting
- patterns
- mass
- radiation
- absorption
- temperature
- climate
- differential heating

Don't Be Surprised

There are several questions in the "purpose" paragraph above. If you were to take a thermometer outdoors with you and take temperatures at different places around your home or school, you might be surprised at the differences you would find. Your students will probably predict double-digit differences but will soon be satisfied with a few degrees. They will be surprised at the higher temperatures near the foundation of homes or on or above patches of bare soil. They might predict that areas protected from wind would also be warmer than open spots but not that temperature readings high above the ground may be different than those close to the ground.

Content Background

Climate can be defined as the prevailing weather conditions in an area over a long period of time. People who live in desert areas expect to have warm days, cool nights, low humidity, and few changes in weather patterns over the year. Those in coastal areas expect high humidity and winds that change from offshore to onshore as the day progresses. In extreme southern and northern areas of the globe it is normal to expect cold winters and warm summers. People who live on islands can expect that the surrounding water will moderate the temperature and humidity over the year. Of course there are always exceptions such as storms that bring extremes to any type of climate, but overall, the climatic conditions change very little from decade to decade. On the Earth, there have been dramatic climatic changes over millions of years due to shifting continents and cataclysmic conditions such as huge volcanic eruptions and meteors striking the planet. But, over scores of generations climates remain reasonably steady and predictable.

Within climates however, there are microclimates, which may affect entire cities and counties. San Francisco, for example, due to its proximity to the ocean and warm currents, its hilly landscape, and prevailing winds, has whole sections of the city with different microclimates. San Diego has a similar situation. Cities are a dynamic example of human constructed microclimates. The use of concrete in buildings and streets provides a heat absorbing mass that collects heat and radiates it into the atmosphere. Thus, cities are generally warmer than an open countryside. The Redwoods National Park is located where it is because of the microclimate that provides a daily fog on the shoreline, which in turn provides the necessary moisture for the huge redwood trees, which grow only there. The microclimate around your school or home is not necessarily as dramatic but does provide a surprise to most people who take the time to map the differences in climate in their little piece of the world.

My wife and I added about 50 centimeters of depth in black soil to our raised beds in our New England vegetable garden during the fall months and then added a plastic cover over the bed. We were harvesting lettuce in December even after several hard frosts. The added mass of soil, combined with the trapping of solar energy, warmed the soil the several degrees necessary to keep the environment warm during the cold nights and created a little greenhouse effect and a small microclimate.

You will certainly find areas where there is more sunlight during the day than in other areas. There will be areas where there is more moisture than others. All of these factors will change the climate in those places and provide you with help as well as challenges when it comes to choosing the best place for certain plants. We tend to think of our land as homogeneous when it comes to temperature, humidity, and climate but this is not the case. It may appear from illustrations of the sun shining on the Earth that all areas receive equal heating but the planet is made up of many different kinds of materials and landforms. The same is true of our smaller, more familiar areas. Thus, Andy and Katie found that when the car was parked in the little protected area, the microclimate surrounding the car provided enough heat from the house side to melt the windshield but not the rear window a mere three or four meters away.

We also create microclimates in our homes by insulating walls and roofs and adding humidifiers to increase the relative humidity in the home. Thermostats are placed in strategic places so that they are most likely to record the temperature and regulate the heating system in a comfortable way. One does not, for example, place a thermostat directly over a radiator because that does not give an accurate reading of the general temperature in the house. They are not placed on the ceiling or on the floor for the same reason. They usually are placed at eye level, which is where we generally spend our time.

During the last half of the 20th century and the first part of the 21st century, there has been a great deal of concern about global warming. Due to our industries and automobiles it is feared that "greenhouse gases," mostly carbon dioxide, have put a layer of gas into our atmosphere much like the plastic cover in our garden vegetable bed that is causing the average atmospheric temperature of our earth to rise slowly but steadily. Ice caps are melting and there is fear that the additional water in the oceans will raise the sea level and flood shoreline communities and endanger species of animals such as polar bears in the Arctic. This theory is garnering support by scientists all over the world and if true, global warming will cause megaclimatic changes everywhere.

Most of our weather takes place in the layer of air (the troposphere) that ranges from sea level to about 13,000 meters although some storm clouds can project above that level. But in this story we are concerned about the layer of air just a meter or two above the surface.

related ideas from National science education standards (NRC 1996)

K–4: Changes in the Earth and Sky
- Weather changes from day to day and over the seasons. Weather can be described by measurable quantities, such as temperature, wind direction and speed, and precipitation.

K–4: Objects in the Sky
- The sun provides the light and heat necessary to maintain the temperature of the earth.

5–8: Structure of the Earth System
- The atmosphere is a mixture of nitrogen, oxygen, and trace gases that include water vapor. The atmosphere has different properties at different elevations

5–8: Earth in the Solar System
- The sun is the major source of energy for phenomena on the earth's surface, such as growth of plants, winds, ocean currents, and the water cycle.

related ideas from Benchmarks for science Literacy (aaas 1993)

K–2: Energy Transformation
- The sun warms the land, air, and water.

3–5: Energy Transformation
- When warmer things are put with cooler ones, the warm ones lose heat and the cool ones gain it until they are all at the same temperature. A warmer object can warm a cooler one by contact or at a distance.

6–8: Energy Transformation

- Heat can be transferred through materials by the collision of atoms or across space by radiation.

Using the Story With Grades K-4

Grades K–2 students often have a very difficult time reading thermometers. Their most common experience with thermometers is probably having their temperature taken. Using this story with early childhood students would offer an opportunity to learn about the thermometer and to talk about being hot and cold and what conditions contribute to that feeling. If they are able to use the thermometers they can certainly keep records of the indoor and outdoor temperatures from day to day and use these records to study the variations in readings. The question arises about the use of Celsius scales for young children. It seems that if children can become bilingual they can also become comfortable with two scales of temperature. You must make sure that they realize that the difference in numbers is merely due to the kind of thermometer being used rather than the temperature they are measuring. You should not spend time teaching children how to convert from one scale to another but encourage them to "think" in one scale or the other.

Soon they will see that energy from the Sun causes higher temperatures in sunny places. Likewise, shady places receive less energy from the Sun, so they have lower temperatures. They can be introduced to the idea that the Sun is the source of warmth for the Earth and can verify this with their newly found skills in temperature reading. Keeping a daily record of the weather is a valuable skill, especially if it includes connecting their data to other forms of weather observation such as clouds, precipitation, and overall weather conditions. This story has been specifically tested with third graders and older children with good results.

Using the Story With Grades 5–8

As with any story, the lesson begins with a discussion of the mystery. The students will probably have personal stories that will parallel the experiences of the story characters. Asking the students to tell you what they believe about how temperatures can vary in different places will reveal what kind of ideas they are bringing to your classroom. Your question could be something like, "What could cause the temperatures to be so different at the two ends of the car?" Once their ideas are recorded on the class chart and in their science notebooks, the "I think…" statements can be changed to questions for testing. You may also ask them if they think that there are different temperatures in various places around the school grounds, why they think so and how they could find out. Combining their experiences and your questions should help students develop a series of plans to map the school grounds with thermometers. You may also find this to be an opportunity to combine mapping skills and measurement skills into the unit, thereby integrating your math and science curricula. Once the mapping is done, and they have had a chance to observe the school grounds more carefully, they may be able to develop some hypotheses about where they believe the temperatures might vary. At first, the majority will focus on the sunny spots with obvious results. Remind them by returning to the story that Andy and his sister found that the carport area was not in the sun, yet had variations in the temperature within a small area. This may encourage them to seek out similar spots on the grounds to see if they get similar results. In their science notebooks, they should be describing the areas they are sampling with notations about the shape of landforms, human-made constructions, or changes in the topography and ground cover. They may note for example, that the morning Sun shines consistently on brick or concrete areas of the building and that even later in the day, those spots are still warm even though they are no longer in direct sunlight. This may lead you to gather data in various locations at different times of the day if this variable comes up.

This may also lead to some additional investigating into the heat-absorbing qualities of various materials such as water, concrete, asphalt, soil, grass, etc. Further experimentation on how quickly and how long these materials retain heat will probably result in additional questions and findings. Is there a difference between how long it takes various materials to reach a certain temperature in direct sunlight? Do some materials stay warmer than others over time?

It is important to note that the questions and experiments are now in the hands of the students and their notebooks should reflect this. Remember to ask for statements of support for any conclusions they make. Now, they may be ready to finish the story and you will be ready to see the amount of growth they have made.

related NSTA BOOKS and Journal articles

Driver, R., A. Squires, P. Rushworth, and V. Wood-Robinson. 1994. *Making sense of secondary science: Research into children's ideas.* London and New York: Routledge Falmer.

Keeley, P. 2005. *Science curriculum topic study: Bridging the gap between standards and practice.* Thousand Oaks, CA: Corwin Press.

Keeley, P., F. Eberle, and L. Farrin. 2005. *Uncovering student ideas in science: 25 formative assessment probes* (vol. 1). Arlington, VA: NSTA Press.

Keeley, P., F. Eberle, and J. Tugel. 2007. *Uncovering student ideas in science: 25 more formative assessment probes* (vol. 2). Arlington, VA: NSTA Press.

Robertson, W. 2002. *Energy: Stop faking it! Finally understanding science so you can teach it.* Arlington, VA: NSTA Press.

references

American Association for the Advancement of Science (AAAS). 1993. *Benchmarks for science literacy.* New York: Oxford University Press.

National Research Council (NRC). 1996. *National science education standards.* Washington, DC: National Academy Press.

CHAPTER 8

THE LITTLE TENT THAT CRIED

Splash!! Right in the left eye.

Rani looked up into the darkness inside the tent that was her camping home for the night.

Splash!! Right smack in the right eye this time.

"Okay, who's the wise guy?"

Splash!! Right in the middle of the forehead.

"Okay, that's it!! Somebody is in trouble and their squirt gun is toast!"

Rani turned on her flashlight only to find the tent tightly zipped up and her tent partner, Annie sleeping soundly. At least, she was pretending to sleep.

"Annie, wake up!" yelled Rani as she shook her friend.

"Wha-, wha-, what's going on?… Why are you waking me up, Rani?" said a sleepy Annie.

"You know what's going on, Annie" said Rani angrily.

"Why is water dripping down your face, Rani? You look like you were in a shower."

"Exactly," spat Rani, "and I feel like I was in a shower too!"

Splat!! Right on the pillow behind her.

And now Rani felt a little sheepish. She was looking right at Annie and yet the water was still hitting her bed. She shone the flashlight up on the tent top and there it was, a drop of water waiting to fall on her bed again.

"What do I have to do, sleep under an umbrella?"

"What are you raving about, Rani? It's the middle of the night!" And then Annie looked up at the tent top illuminated by Rani's flashlight beam.

"Oh, no! We have a leaky tent and it must be raining. But at least it's only on one side of the tent. Goodnight, Rani,"

"Oh no you don't, Annie. We share this tent, and if I get wet, you get wet."

"No way! I'm too tired to argue but if you want to slide over to my side, go ahead."

Rani opened the flap on the tent and looked out. The moon and stars were bright, it was cool—but there certainly was no rain.

"There goes that theory," said Rani and snuggled over as far as she could get toward the other side of the tent.

About an hour later: splat! Right in her right ear. This time she was too tired to care and slept the rest of the night.

The next morning, the campers awoke to another hot and muggy day. It had been in the 90s for a week now and it felt like they were swimming in hot air. Rani's pillow was soaking wet and there was plenty of moisture on Annie's pillow as well. Rani had to find out what was going on. It happened that everybody had damp spots in their tents as well. All of their tents couldn't have been leaking and anyway there had been no rain all night. The grass was wet and the leaves on the trees were wet and the inside of all of their tents were beaded with water droplets.

Penny, their counselor, was getting the morning fire started when the girls approached her and told her the story of their wet night.

"That's very interesting," said Penny. "I'll bet you are wondering where the water came from. Do you have any ideas? There has been a lot of humidity lately—you know, a lot of moisture in the air. Maybe it came from there."

Rani and Annie looked at each other. "I certainly didn't feel any water in the air and I've been walking around in it for most of the week," said Rani.

"I really think our tents are leaky," said Annie

"Everybody's?" asked Penny

"Well, that is strange, but where else could the water come from and get inside our tents if there wasn't a hole in the tent?"

"Maybe it came from our breath. You know, like when you breathe on a window, it gets cloudy," said Tom who was standing nearby.

"Yeah, well maybe so, but why did it collect on the tent ceiling and rain on

us?" said Annie, unconvinced.

"That sounds like a lot of magic!" muttered Rani. "Invisible water from the air or our breath suddenly turning to rain inside our tents. I think it's time for a morning swim. At least I can see that water without using my wand!!"

BACKGROUND

Purpose

Rani and Annie experienced the water cycle firsthand or perhaps, "first face" would describe it better! This actually happened to me during a camping trip in Everglades National Park years ago. The humidity was fierce but the air cooled down overnight and I awoke to a wet face and wet pillow. I was not sure whether it was the high humidity of the subtropics, or my breath, or both, but I knew one thing for sure: My pillow and I were wet! This story is designed to help the students see the water cycle in a natural situation rather than in the usual highly stylized manner. The water in their breath or in the air inside their tent in vapor form condensing on the cooler tent surface and returning to liquid form "raining" down upon their bodies is something to which the students might be able to relate directly.

Related Concepts

- Evaporation
- temperature
- relative humidity
- conservation of matter
- condensation
- humidity
- cycle and energy

Don't Be Surprised

Your students will provide you with many interesting opinions about where the water in the tent came from. Very few children in elementary and middle schools believe that there is actually enough water in the atmosphere to cause this phenomenon. Most of the teachers with whom I have discussed this will tell stories of how difficult it is to get the children to believe that the water that collects on the outside of a cold drink comes from the air around it, but would rather believe that the water penetrated the glass from the inside. In the story, Rani is obviously unconvinced that there is water in the air surrounding her and therefore would be resistant to the idea that it could be responsible for the "rain" in her tent. Rani is typical of most children and some adults in this respect. The moisture in breath is easier to believe since we see evidence of this each time we breathe on a mirror or a glass in the fog that is created. Yet, we know that in such instances as the "sweaty" glass of cold drink, the water must come from the air and that it is indeed present. Convincing children is a different matter.

One factor that has added to the confusion in understanding the water cycle has been the traditional representation of the land, water, clouds, and rain in diagrams in many texts that show water going from ponds and lakes, directly up to the clouds and then raining down upon the source again. This oversimplification can cause children and adults alike to believe that the water cycle is a consistent, never-ending transportation from land to cloud to land again. Given the fact that most of our planet's fresh water is tied up in underground reservoirs, ice and in oceans, lakes, and streams, water that evaporates spends most of its time in one of these places or else remains in the atmosphere in our general vicinity as atmospheric moisture. Water in the oceans has been locked in place for centuries and

the same is true for the glaciers and polar caps. The important concepts here are evaporation, condensation, and the conservation of matter despite the physical change in the state of the water in question. A common misconception is that water no longer exists when it evaporates.

However, we must not ignore the part of the water cycle that brings us clouds, precipitation, and the replenishing of the water on our planet, which we need so badly.

Content Background

You may have already experienced a situation like this by finding droplets of water on your ceiling or walls during a particularly humid weather episode. Or you may have noticed fogging windows during a cold spell when you were boiling something on the stove. Another example would be the fogging of the inside of your auto windows on cold days. Contrary to pictorial views of the water cycle in texts, it happens in everyday situations without rain clouds and lakes. You see a form of the water cycle when you, as Tom said in the story, breathe on a cold window and form a fine mist of water on the window. How many of us remember doing that on car trips when we were children and then writing our names (or other words) on the windows, much to our parents' chagrin? Our warm breath containing water vapor loses energy to the cold window and the gas changes into liquid. The gas, warmed by the energy from our bodies, was transformed when it touched the colder window, thus causing what scientists call a "phase change." In this case it is called condensation.

Water seems to be a magical substance that falls from the sky, runs from our faucets, and seemingly disappears from wet clothes and puddles. In order to understand the water cycle, one must understand that water molecules can exist suspended in the air, that they get there through the process of evaporation or the escape of these molecules from the surface of water and that the escaped molecules (vapor) can change back into liquid water again (condensation). All of these changes require the give and take of energy. It takes energy transferred to the water molecules in a pair of jeans hanging on the line to change the water molecules to vapor. It requires a release of energy by these molecules in vapor form to become water molecules again. Both the water molecules and the energy involved are conserved; in other words, neither the mass of the water molecules or the amount of energy in the transfer changed.

First of all, water is a liquid, which means that its molecules are in motion and more loosely held, so that they can roll over each other and therefore fill a container or spill out of that container when the liquid is poured. Sometimes the energy in the motion of a molecule is great enough that it can escape the rest of its neighbors (evaporate) and suspend itself in the air. Here it joins other molecules of water in the air, which bounce off each other and thereby are able to move up into the atmosphere. As it leaves its fellow molecules to evaporate a bit of energy was required to break it loose from its surroundings so that the liquid it has just left which supplied the energy is a tiny, tiny bit cooler than it was before the escape. You may have noticed this when water evaporates off of your skin when you are wet and you feel cooler since the heat from your body has supplied the energy that allows the water to evaporate. This explains the chill and the "goose bumps" on your skin when you get out of the pool.

Second, these molecules of water can change back again into liquid if they lose the energy to another source. On cool ground, high in the sky, on your cool car window, or in cool air, the vapor molecule loses its extra heat energy and returns to a liquid form. If the vapor touches the cooler surface of a tent, it reverts to water, and as the tiny droplets adhere to each other the droplets become large enough that they eventually fall on your face or pillow.

I do not intend to downplay the water cycle that involves large areas of the globe. These are the cycles depicted in most textbooks showing water evaporating from lakes or oceans, rising up to the sky, forming clouds, and raining the original water back down to earth. The basic phenomenon of the water cycle is absolutely essential to the planet. But as depicted, it gives most students an oversimplified view of the ways in which water is recycled. Students may believe from these drawings that water from puddles in Chicago evaporate around noon, go immediately into the sky, form clouds, and rain the same water later that afternoon in Detroit, from which it evaporates again during the afternoon from Lake Erie. Actually that could happen, but in reality water may spend centuries or longer in oceans and we know that some of the ice in the glaciers might be 10,000 years old. When glacial ice melts, the meltwater which is full of glacial debris often goes directly to the bottom of the ocean to remain there for eons before it can rise to the surface and have an opportunity to evaporate. In some cases, the glacial meltwater will mix with surface water but still remains in a huge reservoir of water.

I am particularly fond of a simulation game called "The Incredible Journey," found in the teacher's edition of Project WET (1995). It is a game in which the students act out the journey of water droplets in the cycle, moving from place to place, but often ending up in seemingly endless lines at the ocean or ice cap locations, showing that the cycle is not the idealistic cyclical occurrence that text drawings tend to suggest. You can find this activity on their website at *www.projectwet.org/activities.htm.* Click on "The Incredible Journey." The water cycle is dependent upon numerous conditions, which are the basis for the story and I hope the discussions and investigations that follow.

related Ideas From National science education standards (NrC 1996)

K–4: *Properties of Objects and Materials*
- Materials can exist in different states: solid, liquid, and gas. Some common materials, such as water, can be changed from one state to another by heating or cooling.

5–8: *Structure of the Earth System*
- Water, which covers the majority of the Earth's surface, circulates through the crust, oceans, and the atmosphere in what is known as the "water cycle." Water evaporates from the Earth's surface, rises and cools

as it moves to higher elevations, condenses as rain or snow, and falls to the surface where it collects in lakes, oceans, soil and in rocks underground.

related ideas from Benchmarks for science Literacy (aaas 1993)

K–2: The Earth

- Water left in an open container disappears, but water in a closed container does not disappear.

3–5: The Earth

- When liquid water disappears, it turns into a gas (vapor) in the air and can reappear as a liquid when cooled, or as a solid if cooled below the freezing point of water. Clouds and fog are made of tiny droplets of water.

6–8: The Earth

- The cycling of water in and out of the atmosphere plays an important role in determining climatic patterns. Water evaporates from the surface of the earth, rises and cools, condenses into rain or snow, and falls again to the surface. The water falling on land collects in rivers and lakes, soil, and porous layers of rock, and much of it flows back into the oceans.

Using the Story With Grades K–4

If you can obtain a copy, you might want to begin with using the probe "Wet Jeans" from *Uncovering Student Ideas in Science* (vol. 1) (Keeley, Eberle, Farrin 2005). This could also be used as a pre- and post assessment.

This chapter's story is geared toward students who are at least eight or nine years old. Five- and six-year-old children may enjoy the story and provide you with interesting responses but will very likely be too young to respond to the intent of the story. In fact the Standards and Benchmarks both expect that at the K–2 age level, students should be focusing on the observations of water "disappearing" (evaporating) from puddles and dishes, etc. I have a problem with the word "disappearing," because it often means, "no longer existing" to children. Another definition states that disappearing means, no longer in view, which is more accurate in this case. However it might be best to use an analogy such as: A ball rolling under a chair seems to disappear but it is still there although hidden from view. For the third and fourth graders the Standards and Benchmarks both agree that the concept of water changing to vapor and back again is not too difficult. For the younger students, activities inquiring into the conditions that accelerate or hinder the evaporation of water are useful. You might ask them what things help or hinder the water from escaping from a dish of water. A good question to begin this inquiry might be, "How many ways can we think of to make water evaporate faster?"

You will have to help them identify variables such as the surface area of the dish (shallow water in large dish) or depth of water, (deeper water in a small dish or glass), and keeping the amount of water constant in all tests, placing the dishes or glasses in the same spot, etc. If they look at the process as a race, they can predict from their own experiences and concentrate on making the race "fair." They will find that shallow water and large surface area cause the most rapid evaporation and the idea of a large, shallow, surface causing faster evaporation should not be lost on them.

When using this story with third or fourth graders, you can find suggestions below in the section on using the story with grades 5–8 and modifying them accordingly.

Using the Story With Grades 5–8

As with all stories, after the reading you should ask the students what they know about the problems posed in the story. Write their comments on a large sheet of paper labeled, "Our Best Thinking so Far." When these statements are turned into questions, the students may begin to pose hypotheses to test. All of these steps should be recorded in their science notebooks. If you are comfortable with having several experiments going on at the same time, small groups of students can choose a hypothesis to test and then go about designing the investigation. It usually makes a lot of sense to have these design groups report to the class and ask for suggestions. That way the entire class is involved to some degree in each investigation. Usually students seem to want to reproduce the situation featured in the story. Small tents can be constructed from coat hangers and fabric such as oil cloth, canvas, or rip-stop nylon. It will be necessary to cool off the tent surface; this can be done with a plastic bag of ice cubes hung on the tent surface. Students may want to breathe into the tent to simulate the breathing by the sleeping girls. Some children like to place a saucer of warm water in the tent and let it evaporate. Soon, under the area that has been cooled, water droplets will form, reproducing the situation in the story. In the discussion that follows, you can introduce them to the terms *evaporation* and *condensation*, which will now have a real-world connection.

From the chart you created at the beginning of the story follow-up you will probably have children who will tell you about drink glasses that were coated with water or other experiences with condensation or evaporation. These statements need to be tested experimentally and shared with the class by summaries from their science notebooks. After playing the game "The Incredible Journey" from the *Project Wet* guide, the topic of global water cycles can be visited and at this point, the diagrams of the water cycle can be discussed with experience and knowledge about the concepts involved, evaporation and condensation. Bringing in the points about energy gain and loss can be done with students who have the maturity to discuss such things. At this point however, it is enough that they have had the first-hand experience with the water cycle system and with its component parts.

related nsta books and journal articles

Driver, R., A. Squires, P. Rushworth, and V. Wood-Robinson. 1994. *Making sense of secondary science: Research into children's ideas.* London and New York: Routledge Falmer.

Hand, R. 2006. Evaporation is cool. *Science Scope* (May): 12-13

Keeley, P. 2005. *Science curriculum topic study: Bridging the gap between standards and practice.* Thousand Oaks, CA: Corwin Press.

Keeley, P., F. Eberle, and L. Farrin. 2005. *Uncovering student ideas in science: 25 formative assessment probes* (vol. 1). Arlington, VA: NSTA Press.

Keeley, P., F. Eberle, and J. Tugel. 2007. *Uncovering student ideas in science: 25 more formative assessment probes* (vol. 2). Arlington, VA: NSTA Press.

references

American Association for the Advancement of Science (AAAS). 1993. *Benchmarks for science literacy.* New York: Oxford University Press.

Keeley, P., F. Eberle, and L. Farrin. 2005. *Uncovering student ideas in science: 25 formative assessment probes* (vol. 1). Arlington, VA: NSTA Press.

National Research Council (NRC). 1996. *National science education standards.* Washington, DC: National Academy Press.

Project WET, Curriculum and activities guide. 1995. The Amazing Journey. Bozeman, MT: Water conservation Council for Environmental Education. 161–165.

BIOLOGICAL SCIENCES

Core Concepts	About Me	Bugs	Dried Apples	Seed Bargains	Trees From Helicopters
Animals	X	X			
Classification		X	X	X	X
Life Processes	X	X	X	X	X
Living Things	X	X	X	X	X
Structure and Function		X	X		X
Plants			X	X	X
Adaptation		X			X
Genetics	X		X	X	X
Variation	X		X	X	X
Evaporation			X		
Energy		X	X	X	X
Systems	X	X	X		X
Cycles	X	X	X	X	X
Reproduction	X	X	X	X	X
Inheritance	X	X	X		X
Change of State		X	X		
Genes	X		X		X
Metamorphosis		X			
Life Cycles		X	X		X
Continuity of Life	X	X	X	X	X

CHAPTER 9
ABOUT ME

Vicki loved spending her summers with her aunt Maureen and Uncle Ben. It wasn't so much that her mother's sister and her happy-go-lucky husband were so good to her, although they were. But it was sharing room with her cousin Nan that made the time so extra special. Nan was a very sophisticated 14, two years older than she was, and had wonderful smelling shampoos and conditioners, exciting smooth-feeling creams designed not only for their faces, but for their arms and legs as well. Nan sometimes wore lipstick and mascara, things Vicki was not allowed to have although she longed for them. At Nan's she was not "too young for these things," and

Nan let her use the cosmetics, "sparingly," as Nan said. That meant, until Nan said "enough!"

One rainy day, while there was little else to do, the girls were trying some new makeup in front of the mirror. Vicki noticed that her ears were very different from her cousin's.

"Hey!" she blurted, "your ears were especially made for earrings."

"What are you talking about?" said Nan.

"Well," explained Vicki, "your earlobes hang down. Look at mine, they're attached right to my jaw."

Nan looked carefully from her own face to her cousin's. "So, is there a point to this?" she asked impatiently.

"Why is that?" asked Vicki.

"I probably got my ears from my mother" ventured Nan knowingly. "I've got my mom's ears and I have my dad's eyes. I wish it was the other way around, but I think girls get most of their looks from their mothers and guys from their dads"

"Huh," snorted Vicki. "I wish I had Demi Moore's hair but mine looks more like my dog's. Anyway, maybe you got your long lobed ears because your mom wore heavy earrings. Then she passed that on to you."

"Can you roll your tongue?" asked Nan, demonstrating her U shaped tongue stuck out of her pursed lips. Trying very hard, Vicki's reflection showed merely a tongue, flat as a board, point out at her from the mirror.

"Maybe if I practiced it a while, I could," said Vicki.

"My mom can but my dad can't," offered Nan. "But, I don't know why. Maybe Dad needs to practice it, too"

Vicki looked at her cousin thoughtfully. "How many ways are we alike and different? And I wonder about our parents. Our moms are sisters—are they alike? We ought to do a family tree."

"Yeah," laughed Nan, "we can run around looking our family over like detectives and copying down drawings of their ears. They would think we were weird."

"Not if we were real careful about it and didn't tell them," said Vicki.

"That might be a little hard when we come to the tongue rolling part," Nan chuckled. "Aw what's the difference, we can tell them we are doing some family research. Maybe we can include Gramps and Grammy."

BACKGROUND

Purpose

What child hasn't heard a comment about having some relative's eyes or nose or chin, or even disposition for that matter? Sometimes such characteristics as musical ability or athletic prowess or even sense of humor are added to the list. Just what kinds of characteristics do living things receive from their parents and what kinds of traits do they not? What makes the offspring of any animal or plant have the basic characteristics of the parents? There happen to be a great number of human traits that are inherited from parents that are very visible to the naked eye. In fact, eye shape, ear shape and in particular, ear lobe presence or not, hair color, hair texture (including curly or straight), the widow's peak, and the ability to roll one's tongue are very easy to observe and record. The purpose of this chapter's story is to prompt children to explore traits inherited from parents and grandparents and to realize that they are passed from parents to their offspring.

Related Concepts

- heredity
- genetics
- inherited characteristics
- variation

Don't Be Surprised

The fact that characteristics are passed on from parents to offspring is true in plants and in animals other than humans as well, but for young children the realization that beetles only beget beetles and roses only beget roses may be a concept new to them. Another revelation may be that no two individuals are identical. The story also brings up some major misconceptions about heredity, mostly about a characteristic like the ability to roll one's tongue, that cannot be developed by practice but is inherited. Students sometimes have a rather Lamarckian idea about inheritance. Jean Baptiste de Lamarck (1744–1829) theorized that structural changes in living things could be passed on to future generations, which was a popular theory until Charles Darwin proposed the theory of Natural Selection in 1859 and raised doubts among scientists thereafter. Vicki demonstrates this idea when she says that her cousin's ear lobes possibly came from the fact that her mother wore heavy earrings.

Another idea in the story points out an idea prevalent among children that girls get their traits from their mothers and boys from their fathers. These assumptions should come out when the story is discussed if you help your students see that the various opinions expressed by the characters do not hold water when compared with the reality of a family tree. Another common example is that loss of a limb or change in the body structure of a parent does not transfer to any offspring.

Content Background

Sexual reproduction is the evolutionary mechanism that is most credited for the variations among offspring. Without sexual reproduction each of the offspring would be a literal clone of the parent. This, of course, happens among one-celled organisms such as the amoeba, bacteria, and some simple algae. But when each parent contributes half of the genetic material that engineers the development of the offspring, the possible combinations of the many genes is basically infinite. Prior to fertilization, sexual cells are formed in the male and female which contain half the number of chromosomes (which contain the genes that carry the instructions for developing the tissues and organs in the yet to be formed embryo). When the new cell containing genetic material from each parent is formed, it contains the requisite number of chromosomes and genes, half from the male and half from the female. The chromosomes and genes of this cell are reproduced over and over again as the embryo develops so that every cell in the new organism contains the same chromosomes and genes as did the original cell. These genes direct the formation of organs, tissues, and all of the traits exhibited by the new offspring. How is it then, you may ask, that the liver does not have blue eyes or the big toe, blond hair? By a complex mechanism during the embryological development of the new being, certain genes are turned off and others are turned on, affecting the development of the proper tissues in the proper places. For example, when the liver is being formed, those genes that carry instructions for the development of the liver are turned on and all others are turned off. At the same time, other genes, responsible for building other parts of the body are on at the proper time and those not involved are turned off. Thus, unless errors occur in the developmental process, the new offspring has all of the right parts in the right places as determined by the combined genetic code received from the male and the female parents.

It turns out that for each set of traits, there are two genes that affect each of the same traits. Some genes are "dominant" over others (the recessive genes) which means that when there are two genes for a certain characteristic and they are different, one gene usually determines the characteristic while the other does not. In flowers, some genes for color are dominant and others are recessive. If however, the two recessive genes are present, the recessive color is expressed in the new offspring. When the reproductive cells of the new organism are being formed, the mix of genes on the chromosomes may distribute themselves in a variety of ways and the next generation may be different in certain traits than the parents.

The understanding of genetics is complex and better left for later years, but the key idea here is that each parent contributes half of the new organism's genetic code and this accounts for the fact that Vicki may have her father's eyes, while she may have her mother's chin.

RELATED IDEAS FROM NATIONAL SCIENCE EDUCATION STANDARDS (NRC 1996)

K–4: Life Cycles of Organisms
* Plants and animals closely resemble their parents.
* Many characteristics of an organism are inherited from the parents of the organism, but other characteristics result from an individual's in-

teractions with the environment. Inherited characteristics include the color of flowers and the number of limbs of an animal.

5–8: Reproduction and Heredity

- In many species, including humans, females produce eggs and males produce sperm. Plants also produce sexually—the egg and sperm are produced in the flowers of flowering plants. An egg and sperm unite to begin development of a new individual. That new individual receives genetic information from its mother (via the egg) and its father (via the sperm). Sexually produced offspring are never identical to either of their parents.
- Every organism requires a set of instructions for specifying its traits. Heredity is the passing of these instructions from one generation to another.
- Heredity information is contained in genes, located in the chromosomes of each cell. Each gene carries a single unit of information.

related ideas from Benchmarks for science literacy (aaas 1993)

K–2: Heredity

- There is variation among individuals of one kind within a population.

3–5: Heredity

- For offspring to resemble their parents, there must be a reliable way to transfer information from one generation to the next.

6–8: Heredity

- In some kinds of organisms, all the genes come from a single parent, whereas in organisms that have sexes, typically half of the genes come from each parent.

Using the Story With Grades K–4

I am aware that this story may have more interest for girls than for boys. Modification of the story's beginning and changing the gender of at least one of the characters might be helpful. For example, the story might begin with two cousins spending some time drawing each other in an art activity. The conversation about comparing ear lobes could then continue as written with modest modification of the characters. This would maintain the integrity of the story and its purpose. It is also a distinct possibility that class members may come from families where tracing family traits are impossible. A fictional family tree may be substituted for the children to use.

With young children, the standards suggest that we concentrate on their realization of the variation that occurs among members of the same species. All the children will be familiar with the variation in pets and some may even have had the experience of observing a litter of kittens, puppies, or guinea pigs. Children who live in rural situations will be very aware of differences in farm animals when compared to their parents. If they are very young, they may have new brothers or sisters, or cousins who are close to their age and have traits that can be observed and recorded in their science notebooks. Young children may need a graphic organizer provided for their observed records, which can help them to record the traits of their choice that distinguish one relative from another. You may start out by asking them how they tell their siblings or cousins apart. Accept all answers because they have certainly developed ways and means of identifying differences among their relatives. Listing all of these categories such as eye color, height, hair color, voice, etc. on a large chart can lead to a discussion about how many ways people or pets differ. Their research into their families or pet families will validate the principle of variation and provide data that will build the first step toward understanding the overall principals of heredity as it is studied as they grow and mature.

Using the Story With Grades 5–8

Once again, girls will identify with this story line but boys may have difficulty relating to the characters. I suggest modification if you feel this will be a problem. The discussion that follows the reading of the story will probably not differ much from that held by younger children except for the sophistication of the responses. I would be surprised if the terms *genes*, *DNA*, or even *chromosomes* did not enter the discussion. The popular media have certainly put these terms before the public, and everything from drug commercials about cholesterol to crime dramas will have at least made the terms familiar. Recognition and usage of the terms should not be construed with understanding; as you know, children and adults alike often use terms without understanding. We must pay attention to the research that tells us that middle and even high school students exhibit misconceptions about how traits are inherited. You may want to consider using the Probe, "Baby Mice," in *Uncovering Student Ideas in Science: 25 Formative Assessment Probes* (vol. 2) (Keeley, Eberle, and Tugel 2007) to find out what your students already think about the topic of heredity.

Most of the misconceptions related in the story may be held by your students and the development of a family tree will help point out how these misconceptions do not hold water. All it will take is a few boys who inherit traits from their mothers (or girls from their fathers) to cast doubts on the idea that boys and girls inherit traits only from their same sex parents. Your discussions may also lead you into the areas of inherited diseases like diabetes and sickle cell anemia. They may also realize that there are some sex-linked traits such as pattern baldness and color-blindness that occur. This can lead into the link between reproduction and inheritance which is not fully understood by a large section of our population. Children in middle school may be ready for the concept of probability and randomness in the distribution of genes in sexual reproduction.

If it is possible, I highly recommend the use of the Wisconsin Fast Plants in the classroom. These modified tiny *Brassica* plants (relatives of broccoli, cauliflow-

er, and cabbage) have been genetically designed to go through an entire life cycle from seed to flower to seed in weeks. Students can pollinate the flowers and gather data on several generations of plant characteristics through use of these marvelous classroom aids. They take up relatively little space and require only a growing table with fluorescent lighting and of course, care and watering by the students. These plants allow you and your students to observe what was never before available, several life cycles of plants in a relatively short space of time.

There are a great many ideas for teaching upper elementary and middle school students about heredity but the main purpose of the story is to allow students to confront their preconceptions about this concept and engage in activities that involve their inquiry into the topic. Developing family trees and connecting information about genes and reproduction will provide opportunities for deeper understanding of terms they have been seeing and using superficially.

You might be interested in participating in a genetic database which is run from the internet. In this program, students from all over the world contribute and tabulate data on dominant and recessive traits and thereby are participating in a much larger gene pool with global results. The website is: *http://k12science.org/ curriculum/genproj/* It usually starts in the fall of the year.

related NSTA Books and Journal articles

Bryant, R. 2003. Toothpick chromosomes. *Science Scope* 26 (7): 10–15.

Cowden, N. 2002. The Alien Lab: A study in genetics. *Science Scope* 26 (2): 24–27.

Driver, R., A. Squires, P. Rushworth, and V. Wood-Robinson. 1994. *Making sense of secondary science: Research into children's ideas.* London and New York: Routledge Falmer.

Hazen, R., and J. Trefil. 1992. The code of life. In *Science matters: Achieving scientific literacy*, 224–242. New York: Anchor Books.

Keeley, P. 2005. *Science curriculum topic study: Bridging the gap between standards and practice.* Thousand Oaks, CA: Corwin Press.

Mesmer, K. 2006. Making Mendel's model manageable. *Science Scope* 29 (6): 24–27.

Rice, E., M. Krasny, and M. Smith. 2006. *Garden genetics: Teaching with edible plants.* Arlington, VA: NSTA Press.

Stanford, P., and S. Heinhorst. 1997. A blueprint for our bodies. *Science and Children* 34 (4):12–15.

references

American Association for the Advancement of Science (AAAS). 1993. *Benchmarks for science literacy.* New York: Oxford University Press.

Keeley, P., F. Eberle, and J. Tugel. 2007. *Uncovering student ideas in science: 25 more formative assessment probes* (vol. 2). Arlington, VA: NSTA Press.

National Research Council (NRC). 1996. *National science education standards.* Washington, DC: National Academy Press.

CHAPTER 10
OATMEAL BUGS

Slam! Bang! Slam! "Where is that oatmeal?" thought Emma. "The cupboards are so full of things we don't ever eat, I can't find anything!" Emma pushed things around, took things out, and reshuffled the cupboard looking for the bright red and blue package of oatmeal.

Why oatmeal, you may ask? Well, Emma's mom has the flu and when Emma asked her if she could do something to help, her mom said, "I would love some oatmeal and brown sugar. It is real comfort food when you have the flu. Would you make me some?" Of course she would. Making oatmeal was easy.

Emma knew she had seen the oatmeal box in the cupboard and being a dutiful daughter was leaving no box unturned to find the stuff and cook it up for her mom. Finally, she moved a few boxes of cereal and lo and behold, there it was, tall and round and with the familiar face on it!

The directions were easy she thought as she read them off the box lid. She opened the lid and poured out the white grainy oatmeal into a dish by way of the measuring cups and suddenly saw something move, all by itself. She peered at the oatmeal a little more closely and oops! There it was again, a little black buggy thing scooting around the grains of oatmeal. Then she saw something else—a little whitish, long, thin thing with legs up front was walking around in the oatmeal. There was also a black thing like the first one that looked dead, with no legs or anything. What was she going to tell her mom? She couldn't serve her oatmeal with all of these things crawling around. Who knew how many more of them were in there? Well, she would just have to tell her mom that oatmeal was not on today's menu. She would certainly understand given the circumstances. But what were these things? Three different kinds of intruders were in their cereal. Hmmmm. She poured the oatmeal back in the box and closed the lid and went to tell her mom the bad news. Maybe she could make her something else, like pancakes or waffles, if there were no things in those boxes, naturally. Perhaps her mom could give a clue to what they were later.

Emma's mom was very understanding and opted for a nice glass of orange juice and some dry cereal. Emma went back to the kitchen.

Later on that day, when Emma's mom felt well enough to come downstairs, they opened the oatmeal box and explored the contents of the box together. Okay, the little white thing was still crawling around but now the little dead looking thing was gone and there were two of the buggy looking things crawling around under the surface. Emma couldn't find the dead looking thing but there was a little empty, black bug case that hadn't been there before. Mysterious things were happening. Luckily, Emma's mom was not squeamish and suggested that they keep the little beasts in a small jar with some oatmeal and keep track of them for a while. "Let's see what we can find out by watching them," she said. And so they did.

Background

Purpose

Insects in the classroom are always interesting and easy to care for. Many people have an aversion to insects or "bugs" as they call them. The mystery here has a lot to do with the life cycle of the insect in the cereal and what the various stages were that Emma found in the box. However, it is important that children get to know more about the most populous animals on our planet. It is important for them to understand their life cycles, their behavior, and the role they play within the Earth's ecosystems. Some can be most destructive and yet without many of them we would have no fruit or many kinds of vegetables whose flowers they pollinate, no honey, no beautiful butterflies and moths, no food for many animals and plants, and no decomposing of animals and plants that die. From the pedagogical point of view insects invite inquiry into their behavior, their life cycles, and their adaptations to every climate and habitat known to humans. Get to know them— they are really cool!

Related Concepts

- life cycles
- classification of organisms
- animal behavior
- animal life
- reproduction
- metamorphosis
- insects
- living things
- adaptation
- variation

Don't Be Surprised

Many students are afraid of insects and would rather step on them then study them. They may believe that all insects bite and are harmful. They may also believe that the representative stages of the life cycle described in the story are different organisms. Also prevalent is the belief that only four legged organisms with fur are animals, thus insects are not seen as animals. Another difficulty arises when children are asked to categorize animals into groups. They have to be helped to recognize that organisms with common characteristics are members of a common group and that in this particular case, beetles are related to bees, ants, butterflies, and other insects. By observing a life cycle many of these conceptions can be modified.

Content Background

"Bugs! Yuck!" This response is so common among humans. But without these animals that make up well over a million different species, our world would not be the same.

We have chosen for the lead character in our story darkling beetles, *Tenebrio molitor*, more commonly known as "mealworms." They are named for the larval stage where they look like grubs but are not since they have six legs and move easily through their grainy medium. They are not worms and their nickname, like so many common names, does not do justice to their lineage.

Mealworms can be kept very easily in the classroom. The adult beetles do not fly so they can be kept in an open container in the classroom. Some teachers have kept their colonies for many years. Each child should be given a capped container with some oatmeal or cornmeal and a piece of raw potato or apple and a few beetles or larvae. The students' job is to take care of them, let them out occasionally, and observe them. Plastic containers are best since they won't shatter if dropped—and they will be! Access to magnifying glasses is helpful. Show the children how to hold the magnifier up to the eye and move the object to be viewed up to the eye until it is in focus. They will become enamored by the insects and over time will see the emergence of the larvae, the shedding of skin as the larvae eat and grow, and the pupa formation which darkens and finally is opened by the adult beetle and the life cycle is complete. I have seen this experience produce a complete change of students' attitudes toward small animals with which they are not familiar. They have gone from stomping on them to studying them because of this experience of rearing a beetle and taking responsibility for their "pet."

You will want to acquire more information about this animal and entering "*Tenebrio*" or "mealworms" into your favorite search engine will bring up many sites with information and more ideas for activities. Two of my favorites urls are *www.thewildones.org/Curric/mealworm.html* and *www.enchantedlearning.com/subjects/insects/beetles/mealworm/mealwormlifecycle.shtml,* the first of which is an article reprinted from *The Wild Times Teacher Connection* and the second has a diagram of the *Tenebrio* life cycle.

All in all, I believe you will enjoy the easily kept insect and the children's response to it. I can almost guarantee a value change in students and teachers who are reluctant to work with "bugs" after they work with *Tenebrio*. I would caution you now that any inquiry directed at any living things in the classroom must be accompanied by a strictly enforced rule that no living thing should be harmed in any way as a result of the inquiry.

The mealworm, *Tenebrio,* comes in two colors, black and yellow. They also can be purchased in two sizes, normal and giant. Do not purchase the enticing large sizes if you wish to do life cycle work. They are treated with a hormone that sometimes prevents them from going through their life cycle. Their energy goes into growing to a very large size but they may not undergo metamorphosis. They are fine for behavioral studies, however, and very easy to handle. Perhaps you will be able to find an old copy of the Elementary Science Study manual *Teacher's Guide for Behavior of Mealworms*. It was first published in the late 1960s and is chock full of great ideas on viewing and using mealworms for inquiry studies. If you cannot find an old copy of the manual you can purchase one under the title of *Animal Behavior* from Delta Education. There are also a limited number of used copies of the *Behavior of Mealworms* listed in internet bookstores.

For openers, I suggest that you do not tell the students the name of the animal. Strange as it seems, knowing the name of the mealworm sometimes seems enough for some students and their curiosity wanes. A great way to start with them is to play a little game invented by a former student of mine, Audubon director, Leonard Amburgy. The game is called, "What Can It Tell You and What Do You Want to Know?" After the children are given the larvae, they are asked to observe the animal

and by observing it, find out what it is "telling you?" Only observations are allowed. Here children can be introduced to the difference between observations and inferences. Observations are strictly descriptions of what they have witnessed or observed. Inferences are an attempt to explain what they have seen. Examples: "The bug moves along the edge of the box," is an observation. "The bug likes to feel a connection on its sides as it moves," is an inference. Help the children stick to observations for the time being. Inferences will come later. List these on the "Our Best Thinking" chart and have the students put them into their science notebooks as well. Next, comes the part of the game called "What Do You Want to Know?" Here the students usually ask questions of the insect such as: What do you like to eat? Do you move backwards, too? Do you like dark places or lighted places? How fast can you move? Do you always move in straight lines? These questions will become transformed into their predictions and eventual investigations. Once again issue the warning that no harm must come to the insect in the course of the investigation. "How long can you stay afloat before you drown?" is not an acceptable question. In the meantime, the children will be keeping track of their beetles in their containers and sooner or later the name of the beetle will emerge. They may even discover the life cycle from other sources and can then watch for the changes in their "pets."

The inquiry into the beetle's life cycle and into its behavior patterns can go on for some time and it is not uncommon to see the activity continue, even in an informal way, for an entire school year. All revelations should be recorded on the "best thinking" chart and in the student science notebooks. You and your students may even discover some things about *Tenebrio* that are not found in books. They will teach you a great deal about insects if you let them.

Tenebrio is a beetle because of its structure. It is a member of the phylum Arthropoda; that means animals with segmented bodies, exoskeletons, and jointed legs. This phylum includes crustaceans, spiders, mites, crabs, etc. Within the phylum is the class Insecta, which includes all insects, which have all of the above characteristics and three pairs of segmented legs attached to the midsection of the body called the thorax. Insects' three segments are head, thorax, and abdomen. Wings, when present, may be two or four and are also attached to the thorax. Beetles belong to the order Coleoptera that have a complete metamorphosis of egg, larva, pupa, and adult. Coleopterans have four wings; the top pair is usually hard and covers the entire thorax and abdomen. Other examples of Coleopterans are ladybugs, dung beetles, lightening bugs, and fireflies. The *Tenebrio* larvae and the adults are about 12–15 mm in length.

These beetles are harmless and do not bite or cause any discomfort to the person studying them. They seem to be comfortable being handled gently and have a life cycle that takes approximately a month at room temperature. Their preferred medium is meal or grains, with a piece of apple or potato for moisture. The apple or potato should be replaced periodically before it gets moldy.

Mealworms can be purchased at local pet stores, where they are kept as food for lizards and other reptile pets. They can also be purchased at biological supply houses or on the internet. They are extremely inexpensive and you can easily start your own colony that can exist for years. They provide a highly visible example of an animal with a consistent and predictable life cycle and show all of the characteristics of a living animal. Again, I direct you to the previously mentioned websites for in-depth information on this insect and its classroom use. Even though some websites will offer lesson plans, I truly believe that the students' questions will provide enough guidance for you to conduct real inquiry lessons for as long as you desire.

related Ideas From National science education standards (NRC 1996)

K–4: The Characteristics of Organisms

- Organisms have basic needs. For example animals need air, water and food: plants require air, water, nutrients, and light. Organisms can survive only in environments in which their needs can be met.
- The world has many different environments and distinct environments support the life of different types of organisms.
- Each plant or animal has different structures that serve different functions in growth, survival, and reproduction.
- The behavior of individual organisms is influenced by external cues (such as a change in the environment). Humans and other organisms have senses that help them detect internal and external cues.

K–4: Life Cycles of Organisms

- Plants and animals have life cycles that include being born, developing into adults, reproducing and eventually dying. The details of this life cycle are different for different organisms.
- Plants and animals closely resemble their parents.

K–4: Organisms and Their Environments

- All animals depend on plants. Some animals eat plants for food. Other animals eat animals that eat plants.
- An organism's patterns of behavior are related to the nature of that organism's environment, including the kinds and numbers of other organisms present, the availability of food and resources and the physical characteristics of the environment.

5–8: Structure and Function in Living Systems

- Living systems at all levels of organization demonstrate the complementary nature of structure and function. Important levels of organization for structure and function include cells, organs, tissues, organ systems, whole organisms, and ecosystems.

5–8: Reproduction and Heredity

- Reproduction is a characteristic of all living systems: because no individual organism lives forever, reproduction is essential to the continuation of every species. Some organisms reproduce asexually. Other organisms reproduce sexually.

5–8: Diversity and Adaptations of Organisms

- Millions of species of animals, plants and microorganisms are alive today. Although different species might look dissimilar, the unit among organisms becomes apparent from an analysis of internal structures, the similarity of their chemical processes and the evidence of common ancestry.

related ideas in Benchmarks for science literacy (aaas 1993)

K–2: Diversity of Life

- Some animals and plants are alike in the way they look and in the things they do, and others are very different from one another.
- Plants and animals have features that help them live in different environments.

3–5: Diversity of Life

- A great variety of kinds of living things can be sorted into groups in many ways using various features to decide which things belong to which group.
- Features used for grouping depend on the purpose of the grouping.

6–8: Diversity of Life

- Animals and plants have a great variety of body plans and internal structures that contribute to their being able to make or find food and reproduce.
- For sexually reproducing organisms, a species comprises all organisms that can mate with one another to produce fertile offspring.

Using the Story With Grades K–4

Young children are usually fascinated with the little larvae that move quickly and in seemingly random directions. After hearing the story, they will have many ideas as to what the little critters in the story might be. Be sure to ask them for some reasons for their ideas. They should have the opportunity to give a reason or experience that supports their answer. With very young children you might decide to give them several larvae to keep in a container as described in the explanation section above. One first grade teacher did this and allowed the life cycle to progress so that the children understood the concept of the cycle. Then she had them use what she called "biodrama" in which the children acted out the various stages of the life cycle of egg, larva, pupa, and adult. This added a kinesthetic aspect to their understanding. After this was obtained she had them play the "What Does it Tell You and What Do You Want to Know?" game. The children were apprised of the meaning of observation and made a list of their observations on a chart and in their science notebooks. They were then allowed to ask questions of the larvae and the class worked together on designing experiments to find out the answers. In this way, the children were able to satisfy the Standards suggestions for inquiry as well as the suggestions about life cycles and behavior.

I would like to refer you to two articles from *Science and Children* that might be of use to you in your teaching this topic: "Investigating Insects" by Janice Fay and "Meet the Mealworms" by Teena Staller. They make good reading and provide some interesting ideas for extending the concept.

Using the Story With Grades 5–8

One way to open the class inquiry is to read the story and then ask the students if they have any ideas as to what the bugs in the story were. These will be mostly guesses and then you can introduce them to *Tenebrio* by handing out a few larvae to each child or pair of children and asking them to observe them for a period of time. This is a good time to introduce them to the terms observe and infer. Ask them for their observations by playing part one of the game, "What Does it Tell You? Ask only for observations and this will give you some formative feedback as to their understanding the difference between the two terms. Write down the observations on a chart and have them put these into their science notebooks as well. When these observations have been verified, you can start part two of the game, "What Do You Want to Know?" If the children ask questions of the larvae directly, they can become more at ease with the process. Examples might be, "Do you like the dark better than the light?" Others might be, "How fast do you move?" "What do you like to eat?" These then have to be turned into hypotheses. Here you can put together the observations and the questions to form hypotheses. From their observations, the children may have an idea what the answers to their questions might be. Explain that an hypothesis is based on some knowledge and not just a wild guess. The above question about the preference of light or dark would then become a hypothesis such as, "Given a choice, the larvae will choose dark places rather than bright places." This is testable and groups of children can explore how they will design a test. Once the class has critiqued these, the investigations can be carried out and the design, results, and conclusions recorded in the science notebooks.

Since these animals are misnamed and are not worms at all, an article from *Science Scope* may be of interest to you as a means to extend the concept. "Mealworms, real worms?" describes how one teacher allowed his students to compare mealworms with earthworms and discover the diversity in animals called "worms."

Also, NSTA publishes a book, *The Pillbug Project, A Guide to Investigation*, which uses a different animal but focuses on the same kinds of concepts.

related NSTA BOOKS and JOURNAL articles

Barman, C., N. Barman, K. Bergland, and M. Goldston. 1999. Assessing students' ideas about animals, *Science and Children* 37 (1): 44–49.

Burnett, R. 1999. *The pillbug project: A guide to investigation.* Arlington, VA: NSTA Press.

Driver, R., A. Squires, P. Rushworth, and V. Wood-Robinson. 1994. *Making sense of secondary science: Research into children's ideas.* London and New York: Routledge Falmer.

Keeley, P. 2005. *Science curriculum topic study: Bridging the gap between standards and practice.* Thousand Oaks, CA: Corwin Press.

references

American Association for the Advancement of Science (AAAS). 1993 *Benchmarks for science literacy.* New York: Oxford University Press.

Dyche, S.E. 1998. Mealworms, real worms? *Science Scope* 22 (2): 19–23.

Fay, J. 2000. Investigating Insects. *Science and Children* 38 (1): 26–30.

National Research Council (NRC). 1996. *National science education standards.* Washington, DC: National Academy Press.

Pope, L. 1997. Mealworms. *The Wild Times Teacher Connection* v2n3. Available online at *www.thewildones.org/Curric/mealworm.html.*

Staller, T. 2005. Meet the mealworms. *Science and Children* 42 (6): 28–31.

Webster, D. 1966. *Teacher's guide for behavior of mealworms, elementary science study.* Nashua, NH: Delta Education.

CHAPTER 11
DRIED APPLES

Jose is seven years old. He lives with his sister Maria, his mother, and his grandmother in the city. Jose is a second grader and he loves his school because he has so many friends there. Alex is his best friend.

Jose and his family don't travel much, so he was very excited when his teacher Mrs. Lopez told the class that they were going on a trip to the country. They were going to visit an apple farm. "An orchard," she called it.

On Thursday, the day of the trip, Jose was very excited. The class boarded the bus and drove a long way out to the orchard. There were trees everywhere. All of them had apples hanging on them. There were green ones, bright red

ones, some were even sort of yellow. The children got to pick apples from the trees and put them in boxes. It was fun. When they were leaving, the owner of the orchard gave the class a big box full of apples. There were many different kinds of apples. They had names like Macintosh, Northern Spy, Cortland, Granny Smith, and Delicious.

The next day was Friday. Mrs. Lopez had plates with slices of the different kinds of apples on them. She asked the children to taste them and decided how they were all different or the same. Each child was to try a slice from each plate.

Jose liked them all until he tried a Granny Smith. "Ooh," he said, "that's sour!" Jose didn't want to eat any more so he put the plate with the Granny Smith slices on the windowsill behind his desk. "I'll put the plate on the table later," he thought. And he really meant to do it. But, soon he forgot all about it and at three o'clock the children were all excited about going home and thinking about the fun they were going to have over the weekend. Jose forgot all about the plate of apple slices.

On Monday, Jose and his friends came back to their classroom and began their day. At snack time, Jose suddenly remembered his apple slices he had left on the windowsill. They were still there, right where he had put them. But, they were different. They were all brown. Not only that but they were shriveled up and wrinkled. He picked one up and it was light, flaky and almost dry.

"What happened?" he said to Alex, his best friend. "It got eaten by mice," said Alex. "But there are no tooth marks," said Jose. "I don't know," said Alex, "they just dried up. Ask Mrs. Lopez."

Jose knew he would have to tell Mrs. Lopez about how he had put them on the windowsill. Maybe she would be angry. But she was a cool teacher and would understand. So he told her and asked her what she thought had happened.

Mrs. Lopez was quite interested and called all of the children around her. They gathered in the meeting area. Jose told them his story and Mrs. Lopez asked them to tell her what ideas they had to explain what happened to the apples. She wrote them down on a big sheet of paper.

Purpose

Water makes up a very high percentage of all living things. This story is aimed at providing children with the opportunity to measure the surprising amount of water found in fruit. It also provides an opportunity for the teacher to emphasize the importance of water in our lives. However, the story is multifaceted and it takes advantage of the curiosity of children about different textures and tastes and encourages them to experiment with foods they are not accustomed to eating. It also addresses the concept of variety in a common fruit, the apple, and could possibly lead to questions about the purpose of a fruit and how it comes to be.

Related Concepts

- needs of organisms
- evaporation
- diversity of living things
- water
- senses

Don't Be Surprised

This chapter's story had its conception while I was participating in a second-grade lesson using students' apple preferences to integrate literature, math, and science. The teacher read the story of Johnny Appleseed to the students prior to their tasting different kinds of apples and graphing their preferences. Some of the students observed that some of the apples seemed juicier than others. This led to a realization that there might be more to the science part of the lesson than just tasting the apples. This story was written and then tested in another second-grade class. Many classes have made "shrunken heads" out of apples by carving faces in the peeled apples and hanging them up until they dried. The effect is dramatic and is a favorite Halloween activity. The dramatic reduction in size in the apples provides evidence of the amount of water in this familiar fruit and eventually in all living things.

For many students, apples are apples and the idea of water making up a substantial part of apples or other fruits is not apparent. The idea that bodies of plants and animals (including humans) are mostly water seems equally absurd! However, making apple cider might be an experience some have had and they know that apple juice has to come from somewhere. Many will not realize that raisins are dried grapes and prunes are dried plums. Since there are ample opportunities for quantitative data, integration with math is a logical connection.

Content Background

If you test various apples you will find that they are quite different in appearance and taste. Some do appear to be juicier and that leads to the question, do some apples contain more water than others? If you are able to borrow a digital scale that will measure with a sensitivity of 0.1 g you may find some differences among the types of apples. But, even with a primitive one-gram primary balance, the weight loss after drying out will be dramatic. The major point is that the apples usually lose more than 80% of their weight when they dry out. Slicing the apples into approximately equal eighths will provide enough exposure and they will dry out nicely in a few days to a week. Apples, as well as all living things, require water to replenish water lost to the environment in many ways. Apples have waxy skin that protects the soft flesh inside from losing water to the air. When this skin is peeled away, the apple responds almost immediately losing water to the atmosphere.

Life cannot exist without water. This is one reason that astronomers and other scientists are trying to find out whether there was ever water on other planets in our solar system. Humans can fast for weeks without lethal results but can last only days without water. It is estimated that the human body is composed of about 66% water. Most students will be amazed at the amount of water lost when a living thing such as an apple dries out. Cells are composed mostly of water and living things are made up of cells. Animals and plants that live in dry climates, such as deserts, have adapted to protect themselves from losing water. Plants have waxy, succulent leaves to keep water from evaporating into the dry air. Animals excrete very little urine and are adapted to obtaining water from the food that they eat. Some animals actually become dormant during dry seasons. Some plant seeds will remain dormant for years until water is again abundant enough for them to germinate. Fish and other aquatic animals lay their eggs in water retaining algae before the dry seasons so that their eggs will live until the next rains fall. Trees such as the bald cypress in semitropical climates, where there are long dry periods, lose their leaves until the rainy season returns.

Since the fruits of plants contain the seeds of the next generation, plant adaptations strongly protect these seeds from dehydration. One could almost say that all successful animals and plants have adapted in some way to retain the precious fluid, despite environmental conditions that would steal it from them.

Apples, of course, are the structures that apple trees use to protect and disseminate their seeds, the doors to the next generation. Luckily for us, they also provide us with a delicious repast. This is a definite survival plus for the tree since it means that animals delight in eating the fruit and thus releasing the seeds into the surrounding territory. It is not an accident that the fleshy fruit surrounds the seeds. It is definitely in the best interests of the survival of the plant to have its fruit be an attraction to wildlife, including humans. This information is provided in case you wish to branch off into blossoms, the formation of fruit, and the release of seeds.

related ideas from national science education standards (NRC 1996)

K–4: The Characteristics of Organisms

- Organisms have basic needs. For example animals need air, water, and food; plants require water, nutrients, and light.

5–8: Diversity and Adaptations of Organisms

- Millions of species of animals, plants, and microorganisms are alive today. Although different species might look dissimilar, the unity among organisms becomes apparent from the analysis of internal structure, the similarity of the chemical processes, and the evidence of common ancestry.

related ideas from BenCHmarks for SCienCe Literacy (aaas 1993)

K–2: Cells

- Most living things need water, food, and air.

6–8: Cells

- About two thirds of the weight of cells is accounted for by water, which gives cells many of their properties.

Using the Story With Grades K–4

After the story has been read to the students, they will have various ideas about why the apples shriveled, dried up, and lost weight. After you have recorded these ideas, there are two questions that usually come up: "Where has the juice in the apple gone?" and "Does the type of apple make a difference in how much juice is lost?" We have found that a good way to begin is to recreate the situation portrayed in the story and have several types of apples to taste. There may be an excursion into where the juice has gone. See the story, "The Little Tent That Cried" (Chapter 8) for suggestions on exploring evaporation.

Then it becomes time to design a way to find out if there are differences in weight loss among the apples. Although children need help in thinking of all of the variables, they will probably insist that all of the apple slices weight the same. This can be accomplished by paring the slices down to a common size and weight. They may also want to know if half an apple will dry out as fast as a small slice, or if a peeled apple specimen will dry out faster or more than an intact section. Remember to ask for reasons when they make a prediction. All records should be kept in their science notebooks. At this grade level we find that drawings are a favorite way for students to keep records. Try to help them to use good labeling techniques so that they will remember what their drawings mean later. If students are disappointed if they do not find large differences in the various apple weight loss, be sure to tell them that they have found an answer to their questions and sometimes the answer is not what they had hoped. Above all, the students are guaranteed to find a tremendous weight loss overall and this should be stressed, because it is important for them to realize how much of the body weight of living things is composed of water. Some students may recall seeing dried up bodies of animals such as frogs or toads. These experiences will add to their realization that all living things consist mainly of water.

These experiments may lead to the application of this knowledge including the making of applesauce and the fact that grocery shelves are full of juices made from just about any fruit imaginable. You may have to help them to realize that fruit juices are really water with flavor from the essence of the individual fruit. Many students have had the experience of mixing concentrates with water to make juice. This may help them to make the connection.

Using the Story With Grades 5-8

Changing the age and grade level of Jose might be a good place to start when using this story with older students. Feel free to modify the story in any way that would make it more appealing to your grade level. Trying different types of apples is still an enjoyable activity for older students and the apple weight loss should still be somewhat mysterious to your students regardless of their experience. With older students, the measurement of weight loss should present few problems. I still suggest starting with an "Our Best Thinking Until Now" chart in order to get students ideas out in the open. Changing these statements to questions and then to predictions is standard procedure in all of the stories. Be sure to require a reason for each prediction so students realize that predictions are not merely wild guesses. Designing the investigations to test these predictions should be done carefully and slowly, involving the whole class taking part in critiquing the designs of smaller groups who are carrying out specific investigations.

Students of this age often wonder if the weight loss seen in apples is also true of other fruits such as pears, oranges, bananas, cherries, etc. Many will have either seen or tried dried fruits as part of trail mixes or granola-type cereals. Drying and comparing these other fruits can be accomplished slowly without special equipment or more quickly in a commercial fruit dryer. Perhaps one of your colleagues has one that can be borrowed. This method of preserving food has been used for centuries before the invention of refrigeration. As you can see, this area of questions has few limits and can proceed as far as you are willing to take it, acting upon the limits of student interest. These activities and experiments fall within the category of the "What would happen if…" or, "I wonder if…" type questions that are so productive. Encouraging your students to pursue these types of questions leads to true inquiry. It is also a wonderful opportunity for you to integrate math and science in calculating the percentages of water in various fruits, which connects nicely to the use of mathematics as described in the 5–8 NSES inquiry standards.

RELATED NSTA BOOKS AND JOURNAL ARTICLES

Driver, R., A. Squires, P. Rushworth, and V. Wood-Robinson. 1994. *Making sense of secondary science: Research into children's ideas.* London and New York: Routledge Falmer.

Keeley, P. 2005. *Science curriculum topic study: Bridging the gap between standards and practice.* Thousand Oaks, CA: Corwin Press.

Keeley, P., F. Eberle, and L. Farrin. 2005. *Uncovering student ideas in science: 25 formative assessment probes* (vol. 1). Arlington, VA: NSTA Press.

Keeley, P., F. Eberle, and J. Tugel. 2007. *Uncovering student ideas in science: 25 more formative assessment probes* (vol. 2). Arlington, VA: NSTA Press.

references

American Association for the advancement of Science (AAAS). 1993. *Benchmarks for science literacy.* New York: Oxford University Press.

Pollan, M. 2001. *Botany of desire.* Toronto: Random House.

National Research Council (NRC). 1996. *National science education standards.* Washington, DC: National Academy Press.

CHAPTER 12
SEED BARGAINS

Jimmy and Jeanine were twins. Not that you could really tell by looking at them. Jimmy was blond and blue eyed while Jeanine is dark haired and dark eyed. But they were twins, born about one minute apart. Jeanine was the first one born and she never let Jimmy forget that she is his "older" sister. They were both in the third grade and in the same class, Mr. Scott's class, and they both thought he was cool. In fact, they thought that third grade was cool. They could read well and Mr. Scott let the class do special projects by themselves because he said they were "mature" kids.

Mr. Scott had started a unit on plants and Jimmy and his partner George had chosen to do something

with seeds. Jimmy was elected to get the seeds for the project and got his mom to drive him to the Pioneer Valley Garden Center to get some "good ones." Jeanine went along for the ride after school because she wanted to get some catnip for their cat. Jimmy went to the display where the seeds were located and found some black-eyed peas that looked interesting.

"I'll take these," said Jimmy to his mom. "There are about fifty of them so that should be plenty for any experiments George and I want to do."

"Looks good to me," said Mom, "and they are only $3.99."

They bought the seeds and Jimmy looked at the

brightly colored package with the picture of the beans looking healthy and green. "I hope our plants look like these."

Jeanine got Mom to pay for the catnip plant for her pet and they left the Garden Center and got into the car.

"I've got to stop at the supermarket to get something for supper," said Mother. "Do you want to come in?"

Both children decided to join her in hopes that they might be able to talk Mom into getting some ice cream as well. Soon they were following her up the aisles as she did her shopping.

Suddenly, Jeanine yanked on Jimmy's collar as he went by and said, "Hey little brother, look at this. Here are your beans without the fancy package."

Jimmy stopped and looked at the package of black-eyed peas Jeanine held in her hands. They looked the same but the package was much bigger. "That's more than we need," he said.

"What did you pay for yours?" asked Jeanine.

"$3.99 plus tax," answered Jimmy.

"Well," said Jeanine, "This looks like twice as many and they are only 99 cents."

"One pound," read Jeanine from the package. "Why didn't you get these instead?"

"I don't know," he answered. "Wait until I ask Mom."

"I guess these are cheaper for a reason," said Mom after the two children had asked her their question. "But, I don't know what that reason is. Let's buy this package for 99 cents and go back to the Garden Center and ask them."

A quick drive brought them back to the Center and within seconds Jimmy was asking the clerk why there was such a price difference in the two packages.

"Well," said the clerk, "I think that the ones we sell are probably better because they're raised specifically for planting. The others are raised for food. Otherwise, we wouldn't charge that much more. Ours must be better."

"What kind of better?" said Jimmy. "Will yours grow faster or what? How do you know they're better?"

The clerk asked some other folks from the Center but all he got in return was that everybody thought that the Garden Center's seeds were "better."

"Gee, we're not even sure what *better* means," said Jeanine. "I'll bet I could figure how to find out though."

"Yeah," said Jimmy, "maybe George and I can figure out a way to test these seeds. And that could be a neat science project!"

Purpose

Children as well as adults are usually intrigued by the ideas of bargains. More seeds for less money is often enough to convince them to buy a larger, cheaper package. In this case, the children are savvy enough to question the value of either package. One seems overly expensive and the other too good to be true. Another common response among consumers of any age is that the more something costs, the better it must be. Implicit in this story is the question, "Which package is the best value?" This story presents a case and an opportunity for promoting the development of alert skepticism as young consumers. This attitude is also important in developing good science habits. It differs from cynicism in that cynicism usually expects fraud or the negative side of any argument to be dominant. Alert skepticism merely suggests that each argument be carefully weighed and that data support any position. In the case of the seeds, the story children ask the right questions: "Why is there such a difference in the prices of the two packages?" and "What are the differences between the two kinds of seeds, if any?" Implied is the question to the seed store salesperson, "Why do you charge more for your seeds?" And finally, "What do you mean by *better* and can you tell me specifically what *better* means?" The story then suggests that the children can find out for themselves what differences, if any, there are between the two groups of seeds. In addition, it asks the children to decide what "better" might mean. It becomes their task to create the criteria upon which they will design their investigations and their predictions.

Related Concepts

- germination
- plants
- life cycles and seeds
- living things
- needs of living things
- experimental design

Don't Be Surprised

Although planting seeds and seeing plants as a result is a common experience for children, they still have a problem seeing seeds as a plant, complete with food enclosed in the package for giving the seed nutrition until it germinates and begins producing its own food. They often benefit greatly from "looking inside" a well-soaked lima bean and seeing the embryo of the bean plant. Since the story focuses on experimental design, you may be surprised how meticulous your students will be in order to design a fair test for their plants. Since they have yet to decide what they mean by "better," they may need help in looking at variables in plants as they grow and be reminded of the importance of the germination ratio.

Content Background

Seeds that are harvested strictly for planting are usually chosen for their viability and are grown for the purpose of planting in gardens or farms. Commercial seed producers avoid any chance of cross-pollination by isolating different varieties of plants and hand pollinating them. Sometimes they are kept away from pollinating insects under nets or in greenhouses. They also keep them away from different types of plants by keeping them at least a mile away from other types of plants, beyond the distance that the average bees fly. Seeds harvested for food are harvested in bulk and are not expected to give genetically pure offspring if planted. Seeds raised for planting are bred for their resistance to disease and hardiness to inclement weather. Their genetics are closely controlled, so that there is very little, if any, variation among the seeds and the resulting plants.

Besides these opportunities to learn more about asking good questions and designing and carrying out investigations, there are a great many opportunities to learn about the germination of seeds, the growth of seedlings, and the conditions for growth. In addition, there are many questions that can arise concerning the planting of seeds and the growth patterns of the seedlings as they mature. Results may differ. Sometimes, the germination rate of the grocery beans is low; sometimes there is no difference between seed types. Sometimes, there are many broken beans in the grocery package and sometimes very few. This means that you are really experiencing inquiry since the outcome for your class may be unique. It is also difficult to find second-hand information about this topic so the students' data are original and there are no set expectations to guide their work. You can also be involved since you do not have a hidden agenda for final conclusions except for the design of the investigation.

The cotyledon(s) are the first leaves to be seen as the plant breaks the surface. These are also called seed leaves and begin the photosynthesis process for the young plant. Seeds also include a substance called endosperm, which provides nutrition to help the plants begin their germination. Plants are known as producers since they are the only living organisms that produce food from the carbon dioxide in the air with the energy from the Sun and the help of a substance called chlorophyll. Animals that eat plants and each other are known as consumers. Almost all of the energy that exists in the world can trace its origin back to the Sun and sunlight's interaction with green plants.

RELATED IDEAS FROM NATIONAL SCIENCE EDUCATION STANDARDS (NRC 1996)

K–4: The Characteristics of Organisms
- Organisms have basic needs. For example, plants require air, water, nutrients and light.
- Each plant or animal has different structures that serve different functions in growth, survival, and reproduction.

K–4: Life Cycles of Organisms
- Plants and animals have life cycles that include being born, developing into adults, reproducing and eventually dying. The details of this life cycle are different for different organisms.
- Plants and animals closely resemble their parents

5–8: Life Cycles of Organisms

- All organisms must be able to obtain and use resources, grow, reproduce and maintain stable internal conditions while living in a constantly changing external environment.

related Ideas from Benchmarks for Science Literacy (aaas 1993)

K–2: Cells

- Most living things need water, food and air.

K–2: Flow of Matter and Energy

- Plants and animals both need to take in water, and animals need to take in food. In addition, plants need light.

K–2: The Designed World

- Most food comes from farms either directly as crops or as animals that eat the crops. To grow well, plants need enough warmth, light, and water.

3–5: Flow of Matter and Energy

- Some source of energy is needed for all organisms to stay alive and grow.

3–5: The Designed World

- Some plant varieties and animal breeds have more desirable characteristics than others, but some may be more difficult or costly to grow.

6–8: Flow of Matter and Energy

- Food provides the fuel and building material for all organisms. Plants use the energy from light to make sugars from carbon dioxide and water. This food can be used immediately or stored for later use.

6–8: The Designed World

- People control the characteristics of plants and animals they raise by selective breeding and preserving varieties of seeds (old and new) to use if growing conditions change.

Using the Story With Grades K–4

A good way to start is by giving the probe "Needs of Seeds" from *Uncovering Student Ideas in Science*, (vol. 2) (Keeley, Eberle, and Tugel 2007). This will provide you with valuable information about what kinds of prior conceptions your students bring to class.

When we have used this story with children in a classroom, we usually have the two packages of seeds to show the class. In addition, we have milk cartons, cups or other containers, and potting soil for the upcoming experiments on hand. It is important that the containers be the same shape, composition, and size. It is just as important that the potting soil be the same brand if more than one bag is used. If you want to create a situation where the children have to argue about controlling variables, have some materials that are different in some ways. In this way, the students will have the opportunity to discuss with their peers the importance of controlling variables in experiments. Once these discussions have occurred, it is usually enough to heighten their awareness for controlling other variables. If they forget some, a few well-placed questions about a variable will help them to remember.

The third- and fourth-grade students we have worked with immediately saw the potential for the experiment. It is, in essence, an opportunity to pit one group of seeds against another—a race or a contest. But it must be fair and children, who play games, know at an early age what "fair" means. You can help them to see that "fairness" is important in this contest as well as in their games. No seed or group of seeds should have an unfair advantage over the others. Thus, you may be overwhelmed by demands that all materials and conditions be exactly the same. This shows that they are taking the investigation seriously.

There are many questions that will come up or perhaps will need you to point out. For example, the seed packet will suggest appropriate depths for planting the seeds. What happens if you plant them deeper? Shallower? Upside down? Is there an up and down position? Sometimes these can be tested in a plastic bag garden. Directions describing the plastic bag seed germination set-up can be found at *www.iit.edu/~smile/bi9404.html*. There are any numbers of variables available to you in using this technique. For a great article about seventh graders learning about plants and seeds see Donna West's article "Bean Plants: A Growth Experience," in the April 2004 issue of *Science Scope*. Even though it is about seventh graders, it has much to offer teachers of any grade level.

You can expect some obvious differences in the results of this activity using the two kinds of seeds. Seeds found in the stores destined for soups and stews are often broken and treated harshly in harvest and packaging. Your students will find many seeds without coats or are damaged and unusable. The students will have their first decision to make about choosing seeds from the less expensive package that appear to be most healthy. But, at the same time it will raise the question about which is the "best buy." Were all of the seeds in the planting package in good shape? What was the ratio of usable seeds from one package to the other? Then, what will be the germination rate? Will one set of seeds germinate first? This latter question will have to be decided by making an operational definition. For example, the question arises, "When do we say the new plant has emerged? When the dirt parts to make way for the plant? When the first green stalk is seen?" These definitions are necessary if group data are to be compiled. Other questions may be: "Does the germination time make a difference in how good a seed is?" and "How long do we wait to see if the seed is viable before we dig down and see?"

When the seeds have broken the surface, if they are, e.g. legumes, they will have two seed leaves, or cotyledons, visible. What are they and what do they do? What happens to them as the plant grows? Were they inside the seeds before they were planted? Ask your students if they can find a way to look inside the seed or you can suggest that the students soak some seeds and dissect them to see what is inside. As you can see, these types of questions can be answered through second-hand inquiry as well as a result of first-hand inquiry.

The plants can be measured for rate of growth. They can be rated on their looks as spindly or healthy. Which are the first to flower? Each day of observation will bring new questions. These observations and questions should all be recorded in their science notebooks and posted on a poster page, prominently displayed and discussed in scientific discourse. Finally, it may well be that there will be little if any differences among the plants. The conclusion might be that for science projects, the store seeds are just as good as the expensive ones. Often in consumer related tests, comparisons of different brands of paper towels, popcorn, window cleaners, and other products, the advertising hype turns out to be just that—hype. Still, it is a finding and is supported by experimental results.

Using the Story With Grades 5–8

You may also want to start by giving the probe "Needs of Seeds" from *Uncovering Student Ideas in Science* (vol. 2) (Keeley, Eberle, and Tugel 2007). It will let you know a great deal about what your students think about seeds and what seeds need to germinate.

Most of the information given in the section for grades K–4 above will be of value to middle school teachers. I especially recommend the Donna West article mentioned above for great ideas for following up on the initial inquiries with the seeds. At this level you will want to focus on the parts of the plants as they continue to grow and look at the kinds of media in which the plants grow, the amount of light, and the adaptations of plants to their environment. Here also you may begin to introduce your students to the miracle of photosynthesis. I can also recommend viewing the Annenberg channel for an enlightening interview with a student about photosynthesis. It is a must see for teachers who are going to teach about photosynthesis. The address is *www.learner.org/resources/series29.html*. Scroll down and select Workshop 2 for the photosynthesis video. You will have to register on the channel first but this is free. Incidentally, there are many interesting videos on this site on all topics. These videos are among some of the best aids to teachers on misconceptions and inquiry teaching.

related NSTa Books and Journal articles

Driver, R., A. Squires, P. Rushworth, and V. Wood-Robinson. 1994. *Making sense of secondary science: Research into children's ideas.* London and New York: Routledge Falmer.

Keeley, P. 2005. *Science curriculum topic study: Bridging the gap between standards and practice.* Thousand Oaks, CA: Corwin Press.

Keeley, P., F. Eberle, and L. Farrin. 2005. *Uncovering student ideas in science: 25 formative assessment probes* (vol. 1). Arlington, VA: NSTA Press.

Keeley, P., F. Eberle, and J. Tugel. 2007. *Uncovering student ideas in science: 25 more formative assessment probes* (vol. 2). Arlington, VA: NSTA Press.

West, D. 2004. Bean Plants: a growth experience. *Science Scope* 27 (7): 44–47.

references

Annenberg Foundation. Photosynthesis video. *www.learner.org/resources/series29.html.*

American Association for the Advancement of Science (AAAS). 1993. *Benchmarks for science literacy.* New York: Oxford University Press.

Keeley, P., F. Eberle, and J. Tugel. 2007. *Uncovering student ideas in science: 25 more formative assessment probes* (vol. 2). Arlington, VA: NSTA Press.

National Research Council (NRC). 1996. *National science education standards.* Washington, DC: National Academy Press.

West, D. 2004. Bean Plants: a growth experience. *Science Scope* 27 (7): 44–47.

CHAPTER 13
TREES FROM HELICOPTERS

Helicopters! That's what they looked like. She had seen them before but this spring, Sarah was completely fascinated by the little spinning objects falling out of the sky and landing on the porch. There were many hundreds of them. She and her brother had been given the task of sweeping them off the porch.

"Not on the ground. Not in the garden. We don't want a bunch of trees growing in our flower beds." Sar-

ah's older brother Eric, who had received them from their mother, gave these warnings.

"What kind of trees do they grow up to be?" asked Sarah.

"Well, they fall out of maple trees so they must become mighty oaks, I guess," teased Eric.

"Come on Eric, how do you know they fall out of maple trees?" asked Sarah.

"Well, my first clue was seeing them there on the

maple trees," said Eric pointing up to the overhanging branches of the red maple.

"I guess I never noticed them on the trees." As she watched, a small breeze rippled through the tree and several of the little flyers began to swirl to the ground, spinning merrily all the way down looking like little helicopters.

"Do all trees make these?" asked Sarah.

"Of course not! Oak trees make acorns and uh, other trees make, uh, their own kind, I guess," stumbled Eric. He wasn't sure about this fact but had to keep his big brother know-it-all image.

"Funny, I never thought about trees making seeds," Sarah thought to herself, being careful what she said out loud to her brother. "I wonder if trees have flowers, too."

"Could I grow a maple tree on purpose—you know, like in a pot?" asked Sarah. "Or, an acorn?"

"Nah," Eric said. "I seem to remember my biology teacher saying that some seeds need to get frozen or cold or something before they could sprout. Acorns especially I think, or some acorns—I don't remember exactly." They continued sweeping and the conversation stopped.

"What other seeds grow on trees?" asked Sarah later when her mother was tucking her in a bedtime.

"What?" answered her mother, completely puzzled.

"Eric and I were talking about growing tree seeds, you know, maple helicopters, acorns in pots. And I was wondering what other seeds grow on trees."

"Well, do you want to count apple and orange seeds as growing on trees?" asked Mother.

Sarah stopped and thought before she spoke. "Yeah, I guess so but I never thought much about apple and orange seeds as seeds except for spitting them out." She thought some more. Then she blurted out, "Do they need to be frozen too?"

"Frozen?" mother responded, confused.

"Eric said that his teacher said that some seeds need to be frozen before they can become trees."

"That's a new one on me," said Mother, "We could look it up, I guess. But for now, it's time to get to sleep. We'll talk more about it tomorrow. Good night." And she planted a kiss on Sarah's forehead and turned out the light.

"Good night, mom," and she closed her eyes. But the visions of all those trees growing in pots on her windowsill stayed with her until she went to sleep.

Background

Purpose

This story is aimed at promoting not only inquiry into the germination of tree seeds but seeing trees as typical flowering plants, also known as angiosperms. There is also ample opportunity to take an excursion into fruits and seeds and the germination of seeds.

Related Concepts

- plant life
- adaptation
- reproduction
- structure and function
- life processes
- living things
- germination
- life cycles
- characteristics of life

Don't Be Surprised

The main misconception might well be that the things we call seeds are really fruits. The story characters talk about the maple seeds and acorn seeds to show that children and adults are not aware of the fruits that enclose the seeds. Maple "helicopters" (schizocarps) are fruits, as are acorns (nuts). The seeds lie within and are protected by the fruits. Try asking a question such as, "What is the purpose of the fleshy material around the seeds in a fruit?" Most likely you will receive the answer that the purpose of the flesh of an apple or orange or other fruits is to provide nutrition for the seeds, rather than to entice animals to eat the fruit and distribute the seeds. Children and adults alike are also surprised by the thought of trees having flowers and producing fruits and seeds. Somehow, they don't think of acorns as fruits but more as squirrel food. Maple fruits are merely trouble-causing objects that fall from the trees and have to be swept up each spring. And other than ornamentals, have you thought of trees as having the flowers that are a prerequisite for producing fruits and seeds? Have you ever noticed an oak flower or a willow flower? Have you noticed a willow seed or a poplar seed? If you live in a temperate climate you probably have and never realized what they were. Children and adults seldom think of trees producing fruits other than those they eat and children may find it difficult to depart from the supermarket definition of a fruit. Therefore the fruits of trees and those of shrubs such as milkweed, Russian olive, roses, and sumac are not thought of as such.

Content Background

Seeds are the plants' "babies" ready to produce the next generation. Seeds are usually in a state of dormancy and when this dormancy is broken and the new plant breaks the seed coat and exits the seed, that process is called germination. The group of plants called *angiosperms* is defined by the fact that their seeds are enclosed in a mature, enlarged ovary of the flower that produced them, a fruit. That fruit is often tasty and enticing to animals that eat them and the seeds are dispersed so that they can grow into successful plants. Contrast these with the *gymnosperms* in which the seeds are "naked" and not enclosed in an ovary, thus have no fruits. These are the conifers such as pines, cedars, and most evergreens. Their seeds are found, lying on the scales of the cone. These are, however, tasty enough to entice squirrels and chipmunks to rip into the cones and while eating some, spread others. Experts disagree on whether these need to be cooled so you and your students will be working on the edge of research. Isn't that exciting? You can try both ways and see what you can find out—a true inquiry-based study.

Acorns can come from many types of oaks; white oak, red oak, pin oak, and other species. Maples are also varied and include the red maple, sugar maple, Norway maple, swamp maple, etc. However, the fruits and seeds of each genus are similar. The white oak produces one of few acorns that do not require cold temperatures for germination and its acorns germinate during the autumn of their maturity. The other species require temperatures of at least 0–2° C for a minimum of six weeks before they can be expected to germinate. During this time they become dormant. (Some dormant seeds can remain so for centuries and one seed was reported to be viable after a thousand years in a desert-like climate). Therefore, in the natural world, acorns that require dormancy do not germinate until the spring of the following year at the earliest. Just as we can force bulbs, we can force acorns by placing them in damp peat moss or soil, in a plastic bag or container, and placing them outdoors, in cool climates, or in a refrigerator, which is set at the required temperature. The bag must be left open to allow transfer of gases. Maple seeds do not require cooling and can be planted immediately.

Your students will probably be familiar with acorns and maple seeds if they live in temperate climates. Even in subtropical areas, the swamp maple, the live oak, and swamp oak are present. Since maples and oaks are two of the most common trees in the continental United States, teachers should have little trouble obtaining these seeds. If they are not available, the seeds of any common tree will satisfy the needs of a class wishing to engage in inquiry about trees and their seeds. In certain climates some tree flowers are very obvious and flamboyant. In others they are hardly noticeable. But if seeds are encased in a fruit, there must have been flowers. These types of plants are called *angiosperms*. These plants have their seeds encased in the ovary of the flower and the ovary usually becomes fleshy as in an apple or cherry. Acorns by this definition are also fruits (actually classified as single-seeded nuts), and are so common that they are often overlooked as objects of study. The same can be said for the maple fruits.

I would like to suggest that you read a most enjoyable book on botany, which will broaden your background on this topic. The book is *The Botany of Desire* by Michael Pollan.

A fruit is the ripened ovary of the seed plant and its contents. Thus you can see that this is a botanical definition, not a supermarket definition. Fruits range from what we normally call vegetables to fruits like apples and oranges, berries, tomatoes, cherries, and of course, maple and oak fruits, coco plums, and pond apples. The fruit protects the seeds within it and provides the mechanism for distributing the seeds. You may well ask of each fruit you see, "How do you help the seeds you enclose, get to where they can best germinate and produce new plants? Are you tasty, so that you attract animals that eat you or bury you and thus spread your

seeds far from the original tree? Do you pop open and propel your seeds or do you produce little parachutes so that they can fly in the wind? Are you shaped like tiny helicopters so that the wind can carry you? Do you have a hard protective case so that you protect your seeds from inclement weather? Do you have a Velcro-like surface on you so that you stick to animals' fur or feathers and travel great distances from your mother plant?" Through natural selection, or paraphrased, survival of the fittest, over the eons that plants have existed, the fruits of seed plants have evolved into the most efficient seed distributors. What you see around you today, in nature, are the plants that are the fittest in terms of reproduction. Of course there are also cultivated plants that have been bred by humans to produce what other humans consider the most desirable characters. Excluding the latter, we are left with the plants that have evolved to exist successfully, molded by the physical and biological forces of nature. Take the acorn as an example. If it germinated directly under the parent oak, it would have to compete for sunlight and water. Acorns are rounded and tend to roll on the ground when they fall, thus taking them a reasonable distance from the sun-robbing parent. Willows and poplars have seeds attached to wispy, cottony parachutes, which allow them to fly with the wind to areas distant from the parent plant. Maples and pine seeds have the little wings that also allow them to drift in the winds to distant places.

Some trees have flowers with both male and female parts, others have flowers with only male or female parts and yet others have female flowers on one plant, and male flowers on another. A perfect example of the latter is the holly where only the female plant bears berries but a male plant must be nearby to provide the pollen. Other plants must have insects that frequent their blossoms to spread the pollen from one flower to another in order to bear fruit. Direct evidence of this are plants that are imported from other lands, without their pollinating insects, and therefore never bear fruit.

But when we focus on the tree seed itself, it holds in its tiny form the beginnings of a new plant and the genetic instructions that will make sure that it is a tree. We expect when we plant an acorn we will get an oak tree and not something else. As simplistic as this may sound, it is a basic concept that children need to understand, as we infer by its inclusion in the Standards.

We can also expect that any tree seed, including that of a gymnosperm, will germinate approximately the same way that any angiosperm will germinate. We will see some form of plant tissues that will provide food to the young seedling until it can photosynthesize its own food. We will see primitive roots and stems and it will require sunlight, water, and rich soil to thrive. Only rarely does a seed need sunlight to germinate. It needs only a nurturing environment with moisture and warmth to begin its life as a growing plant. The little plant begins its growth while in the seed and once it germinates, it merely continues its growth. Once it has established itself in a good environment, it is on its own, to grow and produce flowers, fruits, and seeds when it reaches maturity.

Oak seeds, acorns, have nutritional value and have been used for centuries by native people and others who know how to treat them to remove the tannin, which is bitter and prevents the absorption of nutrients in mammalian digestive tracts. It turns out that white oak acorns have less fat content and sprout in the fall so that they are not the best acorns for squirrels to store. If the acorn begins to germinate its nutritional value becomes less. Red oak acorns have more fat but have more tannin and can be stored for the winter, but the tannin will affect the absorption of the nutrients in the squirrels' digestive tracts. As you can see, it is a balancing act as to which acorn provides the most nutrition. The squirrels seem to prefer the acorns that do not germinate immediately even though the tannin makes them less digestible and I suspect, less tasty. But then who knows if squirrels are gourmets.

Molds are a primary enemy of germinating seeds. Rinsing seeds in a chlorine bath can often help prevent the growth of mold, but you will have to be on constant lookout for mold on your germinating seeds and young seedlings during the two to three weeks it might take to germinate. A caution here is necessary to warn you to use the chlorine bath instead of having the children do so for safety's sake.

related ideas from National science education standards (NrC 1996)

K–4: The Characteristics of Organisms
- Organisms have basic needs. For example, plants require air, water, nutrients and light.
- Each plant or animal has different structures that serve different functions in growth, survival, and reproduction.

K–4: Life Cycles of Organisms
- Plants and animals have life cycles that include being born, developing into adults, reproducing and eventually dying. The details of this life cycle are different for different organisms.
- Plants and animals closely resemble their parents

6–8: Life Cycles of Organisms
- All organisms must be able to obtain and use resources, grow, reproduce and maintain stable internal conditions while living in a constantly changing external environment.

related ideas from Benchmarks for science Literacy (aaas 1993)

K–2: Cells
- Most living things need water, food and air.

K–2: Flow of Matter and Energy
- Plants and animals both need to take in water, and animals need to take in food. In addition, plants need light.

K–2: The Designed World
- Most food comes from farms either directly as crops or as animals that eat the crops. To grow well, plants need enough warmth, light, and water.

3–5: Flow of Matter and Energy
- Some source of energy is needed for all organisms to stay alive and grow.

3–5: The Designed World
- Some plant varieties and animal breeds have more desirable characteristics than others, but some may be more difficult or costly to grow.

6–8: Flow of Matter and Energy
- Food provides the fuel and building material for all organisms. Plants use the energy from light to make sugars from carbon dioxide and water. This food can be used immediately or stored for later use.

6–8: The Designed World
- People control the characteristics of plants and animals they raise by selective breeding and preserving varieties of seeds (old and new) to use if growing conditions change.

Using the Story With Grades K–4

You may find that giving the probe "Needs of Seeds" from *Uncovering Student Ideas in Science* (vol. 2) (Keeley, Eberle, and Tugel 2007) will provide you with valuable information on what kind of preconceptions your students bring to your class.

Maple seeds, as many of us have found, can germinate immediately after falling from the tree. Questions will arise about how to plant these "wild" tree seeds and of course, from these questions arise the hypotheses and experiments for which we aim in teaching for inquiry.

Oaks are a different story. If you can identify the white oak acorn they can be planted immediately. The best way to identify them is to identify the tree and harvest acorns from beneath the tree. For your information, they do best if planted about one inch below the surface. They send out a particularly long tap root (7.5 cm,) so should be planted in an appropriately tall container with a hole in the bottom for drainage. When collecting acorns be aware many are not healthy and harbor a tiny wasp larva, which feeds on the food inside. You may ask the children if they think the acorns will float. All will float if the cap is still left on. If you can remove the cap easily, the acorn is mature. A few minutes soaking in a weak bleach solution (1/2 cup of bleach to a gallon of water) will kill any mold that may be on the acorn. (Caution! The teacher should do this.) When they have made their predictions, put the acorns in a container of water and you will see that some will float and others will sink. The sinkers are the viable ones; the floaters have lost much of their mass due to infestation or lack of a viable seed and the food reserve for the young seedlings. You may want to cut them open and see what is inside and should be rewarded with some insect larvae or other organisms that are eating away at the nutritious food. The sinkers are dense with a seed and food and should germinate. These can also be cut open and it is much easier to do so if they are soaked over night. In fact, when you are ready to plant acorns, it is a good idea to soak them overnight as well. With young children, you may want to place your chosen seeds in a wet paper towel and place them in an open plastic bag so that the children can check on them periodically to see what is happening to the germinating seeds.

One does not necessarily have to stick to the germination theme if the students become interested in, for example, which acorns do squirrels prefer, or more appropriately, do squirrels prefer one or two acorns over others? Also, students may wonder what is inside the acorn and when dissected, they may find a whole community of living things. Their interest may also shift to the seeds of the gymnosperms or so-called conifers and their naked seeds. You may be amazed at the number of questions about these everyday items that will arise once they are involved in dialog about them. How are cones different from fruits? Do pine seeds need to be cooled like acorns? What kind of soil do they like best? How are they different from seeds that are found in fruits? How long does it take for various seeds to germinate? How deep should we plant them and in what position? What is the purpose of the little cap on the acorn? Do we need to plant the cap too? The questions can be endless and with your help the students can design many experiments and learn a great deal about these everyday, yet mysterious objects. Remember, since experts still disagree on exactly how to germinate tree seeds, your students may well be collecting data on questions that are still open.

Using the Story With Grades 5–8

I advise teachers of these grades to read the above passages on grades K–4 since many ideas may be common to both levels. Also some of the techniques mentioned will be important for you to know. Students of this age may have more sophisticated questions to place on the class chart and may be able to develop

more sophisticated experiments. You will also find that giving the probe "Needs of Seeds" from *Uncovering Student Ideas in Science* (vol. 2) (Keeley, Eberle, and Tugel 2007) will provide you with valuable information on what kind of preconceptions your students bring to your class. Testing with this probe has taught us that some students will say that seeds need food to germinate because they are aware of the nutritional substance in the seed as food. Probing will tell you if they are thinking of this kind of food or additional food that has to be added.

One question that may come up is, "What kinds of acorns do animals prefer to eat?" Your students can design experiments, which involve placing several kinds of acorns in an area and keeping data on which kind are taken. Be sure to use only viable acorns since animals usually do not take acorns that are not healthy. This might best follow a dissection of seeds so that your students can discover that some acorns have inhabitants and are damaged. While dissecting a mature acorn you may want to soak the nut in water overnight to make the dissection easier. Look for the plant inside by making a longitudinal cut. This should be done by adults, in a manner that will not let the round nut turn and injure them. It is also a good idea to consider gently using a nutcracker to get the tough outer coat of the nut broken and open for business.

The main question to be asked of the fruit you see is, "How do you help the seeds you enclose, get to where they can best germinate and produce new plants?" Secondary questions would be, "Are you tasty, so that you attract animals that eat you or bury you and thus spread your seeds far from the original tree? Do you pop open and propel your seeds or do you produce little parachutes so that they can fly in the wind? Are you shaped like tiny helicopters so that the wind can carry you? Do you have a hard protective case so that you protect your seeds from inclement weather? Do you have a Velcro-like surface on you so that you stick to animals' fur or feathers and travel great distances from your mother plant?" You may remember the technique described in background material of the story "Oatmeal Bugs," specifically the game "What Does it Tell You, What Do You Want to Know?" It would work well here as well.

If there are oaks and maples near your school and they have low branches you may be able to see the flowers on the trees on a ten minute field trip. In maples, the flowers often appear in the spring before the tree has leafed out and will give the tree a red lacey kind of appearance. Oaks will produce their flowers later and the acorns will not be viable until the fall. Using both trees in your study will test your flexibility in beginning a unit in the fall and returning to it in the spring but it will be well worth the effort.

related Nsta Press Books and Journal articles

Cavallo, A. 2005. Cycling through plants. *Science and Children* 42 (7): 22–27

Driver, R., A. Squires, P. Rushworth, and V. Wood-Robinson. 1994. *Making sense of secondary science: Research into children's ideas.* London and New York: Routledge Falmer.

Keeley, P. 2005. *Science curriculum topic study: Bridging the gap between standards and practice.* Thousand Oaks, CA: Corwin Press.

Keeley, P., F. Eberle, and L. Farrin. 2005. *Uncovering student ideas in science: 25 formative assessment probes* (vol. 1). Arlington, VA: NSTA Press.

Keeley, P., F. Eberle, and J. Tugel. 2007. *Uncovering student ideas in science: 25 more formative assessment probes* (vol. 2). Arlington, VA: NSTA Press.

Quinones, C., and B. Jeanpierre. 2005. Planting the spirit of inquiry. *Science and Children* 42 (7): 32–35.

West, D. 2004. Bean Plants: a growth experience. *Science Scope* 27 (7): 44–47.

references

American Association for the Advancement of Science (AAAS). 1993. *Benchmarks for science literacy.* New York: Oxford University Press.

Keeley, P., F. Eberle, and J. Tugel. 2007. *Uncovering student ideas in science: 25 more formative assessment probes* (vol. 2). Arlington, VA: NSTA Press.

National Research Council (NRC). 1996. *National science education standards.* Washington, DC: National Academy Press.

Pollan, M. 2001. *Botany of desire.* Toronto: Random House

PHYSICAL SCIENCES

Core Concepts	Magic Balloon	Bocce, Anyone?	Grandfather's Clock	Neighborhood Telephone Service	How Cold Is Cold?
				Stories	
Energy	X	X	X	X	X
Energy Transfer	X	X	X	X	X
Conservation of Energy		X			X
Forces	X	X	X		
Gravity	X	X	X		
Heat	X				X
Kinetic Energy		X	X		
Potential Energy		X	X		
Position and Motion		X	X		
Sound				X	
Periodic Motion			X	X	
Waves				X	
Temperature	X				X
Gas Laws	X				
Buoyancy	X				
Friction		X	X		
Experimental Design	X	X	X	X	X
Work		X	X		
Change of State					X
Time		X	X		

CHapter 14

THE MAGIC BALLOON

It was a wonderful balloon! After spending at least 15 minutes arguing about the balloons for Andy's 9th birthday party, Abby and Paul finally agreed on this balloon, which had "Happy Birthday" spelled out in multicolored fireworks on both sides. It was one of those Mylar jobs, which had to be filled with the gas that made them float for weeks. It also made them try to escape into the clouds if you let go of the string.

The lady at the balloon counter attached it to a tank of gas, turned the knob and the balloon expanded and tugged at her hands. The silver envelope filled with the gas and became slick and smooth without wrinkles. "I'll give you lots of gas," said the saleswoman, "so it will last a long time."

"Thanks," said Abby, "It's a present for a birthday party."

"Be sure to hold on to the string tightly," the lady

said as she tied a pretty ribbon around the neck of the balloon.

Clutching the floating silver sphere, the two proudly walked toward the exit with the prize trailing them like a floating dog that had been told to "heel."

It was January and a frosty one at that. Temperatures had been hovering around zero for a week. Abby and Paul stopped at the door and zipped up their jackets and pulled their ski caps down over their ears. Their big sister, Ruth was driving them today and was doing some shopping for herself. Ruth finally met them at the exit door and they all ran through the frosty night to the chilly car.

Once they were strapped in, Ruth started the engine. "Turn on the heat!" commanded Paul in a shivering voice.

"Geez! Wait a bit for this old engine to warm up!" muttered Ruth. "Anyway, with this old car, we'll be home before it gives off any heat." Ruth had just earned her driver's license and their parents were allowing her to use their older car. It had its problems, one of which was a poor heater. But it ran, and it was a safe car.

Abby, holding onto the balloon, glanced up at it as they pulled out of the parking lot and onto the main road.

"Uh, oh!" she said. "We got a bad balloon! It must be leaking." At the next red light, Ruth turned around and saw that the balloon was all crinkly and was not floating like it had before. Paul too, looked disappointed at its condition.

"Better take it back now," he said. "We'll never get to come back again tonight and the party's tomorrow."

"Oh, all right," said Ruth as she reluctantly turned the car around and started back to the mall. In a few minutes they were back and Ruth decided to double-park at the entrance while Paul and Abby returned the balloon. It looked pretty sick by now.

The two children made their way back to the counter but the saleswoman was not there. They looked up at the deflated balloon. They looked at some other balloons they might substitute for the deflated one and after about five minutes, she returned.

"Can I help you with something?" she asked.

"Our balloon is leaking," said Abby.

"Yeah," added Paul. "We'd like a new one."

The woman looked at the balloon and said, "What's wrong? It looks perfectly fine to me!"

Paul and Abby looked up and to their utter amazement saw that she was right. The balloon was as full and plump as it had been when they bought it.

"But, but..." stammered Paul. "Just a while ago it was half flat looking and wrinkled and it wasn't floating or..."

"Did you take it outdoors?" interrupted the lady.

"Sure, we were taking it home," offered Abby.

"That may be a clue to what happened," said the lady winking at them. "Trust me, take it home and see what happens. You won't be disappointed. It's a magic balloon that is always plump when it is indoors."

Reluctantly, the two children went out to the car. Abby turned to Paul and said, "I don't buy the magic stuff, but it sure did leak and refill again once we went inside. What could happen to the stuff inside to make it shrink?"

"At least it seemed to shrink!" said Paul puzzled. "Let's take it home and see

what happens. She said to trust her."

With that, the two got into the car and Ruth drove them home. They watched the balloon very carefully the rest of the trip and well into the evening and again the next morning.

Background

Purpose

This is a story that has meaning for anyone who has ever seen a parade with floating balloons or has gone to a celebration where balloons were present. Floating always seems like magic because it appears to be defying the law of gravity. The helium filled plastic envelopes that reach for the heavens fascinate babies to adults. For this story, the main purpose is to explore the relationship between temperature and pressure of gases but it may spill over into the concepts of floating and density in older children. It also asks questions about gas being a form of matter that has mass and takes up space. Basically, it revolves around a law developed by French chemist/physicist Jacques Charles in 1787 now known as Charles' Law. We'll take a look at how it explains a lot of apparent mysteries concerning balloons and objects that float in the air and hope it stimulates your students to ask a lot of good questions about this phenomenon. Incidentally, in 1783 Jacques Charles ascended to the altitude of 914 meters in a hydrogen balloon of his design. When he landed just outside of Paris, terrified peasants destroyed his balloon. Fortunately, he wasn't hurt. Here was a man, way ahead of his times!

Related Concepts

- forms of matter
- volume
- density
- temperature
- gases
- float and sink
- forces
- energy

Don't Be Surprised

Most children and even some adults have a difficult time understanding that gases take up space and that they have mass. They seem to understand that the balloon inflates due to the increase in the amount of air you blow into it or helium that is put into it. Many will balk at the idea that "free" air around them has mass since they walk around in it all day and don't feel its impact on their bodies. They may believe that the gas is warmer since they have been told so often that warm air rises.

In the literacy area, I strongly recommend the book, *Le Ballon Rouge* (The Red Balloon) by Albert Lamorisse. The story follows a lonely little boy and a red balloon in their mutual friendship in Paris. There is also a movie from which the book was made. The movie is short and has no dialog. The story is a metaphor for friendship and loneliness and should open the door to a lively discussion, whether read to the children or shown as a movie. It is a classic in either form.

Content Background

If you have ever had the opportunity to experience what the kids in the story have you might have noticed the same reaction of the balloon to changes in temperature. If not, you can make it happen right in your own kitchen and be prepared for what your students bring to your class after hearing the story. If you were to put a balloon filled with any gas, even that from your lungs, into the refrigerator or freezer for a short time, you will notice that the balloon takes up less space; has less volume after being chilled. It is much more fun with a helium filled balloon because it adds the dimension of floating and provides another property to observe. The balloon will not pull at the string as much after being chilled and may appear wrinkled due to the lack of volume the gas takes up in the Mylar envelope. Given that most classrooms do not have refrigerators, you may want to try this story during the cooler part of your school year so that the outdoors can do the cooling. Most students will ask questions about the gas in the balloon and these questions will give you an insight into their preconceptions, most of which will not jibe with the scientific explanation. For example working with the questions raised in the story may give them some insight into the behavior of gases since they will be able to see changes in the shape of the balloons. Most of these observations cannot be explained adequately without accepting the concept that gases actually possess mass and take up space.

Older students may also be more interested in why the helium balloon floats and how much weight it can pull to the ceiling. Others may want to see if they can put enough weight on the string to allow the balloon to float and yet not rise to the ceiling. Can it be done? Try it and see.

Picture in your mind that the balloon is filled with molecules of gas, which constantly strike the surface of the inside of the balloon and push it into an inflated state. When the balloon is subjected to differences in temperature the amount of motion of these molecules changes. For example, when the temperature of the gases in the balloon is raised, the molecules move faster and faster and constantly strike the inside surface of the balloon with greater force and the balloon expands since it is stretchable and pliable. Conversely, when the temperature of the gas inside the balloon is cooled, the molecules move more slowly and thus strike the balloon's surface with a lesser force and the balloon deflates accordingly. This is what happened to the balloon as the children went outside into the cold winter air. It reversed itself when they went back into the warm store and waited for the salesperson.

Students may also wonder why the balloon filled with helium floats on the air in the room. Also related to the inflation size of the balloon is the fact that the balloon filled with a gas that is less dense than the surrounding air will receive an upward, buoyant force on it by the surrounding air and this pushes it upward. By density we mean the amount of mass an object has in relation to its volume. Density is a property of any substance. No matter what the size of a piece of, say, lead, its density is the same. In a larger piece of any given substance, the mass obviously increases but the ratio of mass to volume, or density, remains the same. Think of the balloon and the helium inside it as a closed system. Nothing gets in or out but the gas inside the balloon can exert more pressure on the elastic balloon and make it swell and take up more space. The gas inside can also exert less pressure on the elastic balloon, and make it take up less space. As the size of the balloon/gas system decreases, its combined density increases since it still weighs the same but now takes up less space. Thus, it receives less force in an upward direction and succumbs to the force of gravity. This is the same principle that explains why things float or sink in water. If you have ever tried to push an inflated ball down into the water, you can feel the force of the water pushing upwards. Think of a balloon floating in the atmosphere that is pushing it upward in the same way. The larger the ball, the more force you can feel. Think of the difference between pushing a tennis ball under water and a large beach ball. The secret is in the relationship between the volume and the mass of the object and that of the "liquid" in which it is floating.

Most helium filled balloons will slowly lose helium through the Mylar and eventually lose enough volume so that they no longer float. This phenomenon is something that just about everyone has witnessed but is not directly related to this story.

Hot air balloons follow the same principle. As the air is heated, it expands due to its increased pressure, filling the bag with air. The pressure of the molecules in the heated air is also increased and forces the bag to billow out and take up more space. At some point, the upward force exceeds the mutual pull of gravity and the balloon rises. In order for the balloon to stay aloft, the pilot must also keep the air warm by lighting the flame in the cockpit or basket. Should the air cool and the pressure in the bag decrease, the balloon would slowly sink toward the earth. In fact, when the pilots want to land, they open a valve in the top of the balloon releasing air and decreasing the volume.

Should some of you wish to delve more deeply into the physics of the gas laws you will find some interactive material at the following website: *www.chm.davidson.edu/ChemistryApplets/GasLaws/Gasconstant.html.*

related Ideas From National science education standards (NrC 1996)

K–4: Properties of Objects and Materials

- Objects have many observable properties, including size, weight, shape, color, temperature and the ability to react with other substances. Those properties can be measured using tools, such as rulers, balances and thermometers.
- Materials can exist in different states—solid, liquid and gas. Heating or cooling can change some common materials such as water from one state to another.

5–8: Properties and Changes of Properties in Matter

- A substance has characteristic properties, such as density, a boiling point, and solubility, all of which are independent of the amount of the sample.

related ideas from benchmarks for science literacy (aaas 1993)

K–2: The Physical Setting
- Objects can be described in terms of the materials they are made of (clay, cloth, paper, etc.) and their physical properties (color, size, shape, weight, texture, flexibility, etc.).
- Things can be done to materials to change some of their properties, but not all materials respond the same way to what is done to them.

3–5: The Physical Setting
- Heating and cooling cause changes in the properties of materials. Many kinds of changes occur faster under hotter conditions.

6–8: The Physical Setting
- Equal volumes of different substances usually have different weights.
- Atoms and molecules are perpetually in motion. Increased temperature means greater average energy of motion, so most substances expand when heated.

Using the Story With Grades K–4

Children in the early years normally are not ready for excursions into density but are certainly capable of noticing the difference in the shape and size of party balloons in different temperatures. You may use either helium balloons or common balloons inflated with regular air. If you were fortunate enough to have a difference between indoor and outdoor temperatures in your region in the fall or winter, this would be a good time to try this story. If not, placing the balloons in a refrigerator or freezer for a while will result in the same shrinking. You may get questions about what further heating will accomplish. Holding the balloon in a warm place will have an effect as well. You might hold it carefully over a warming plate (careful, not too close!) or hold it under a stream of warm water. Younger children, though they have a difficult time believing that air has mass and takes up space around them, are ready to accept that a gas will blow up a balloon and that it is inside the balloon. It is possible, but difficult to weigh an air-filled balloon before and after inflation on a scale such as a triple beam balance. The difference will be small but it does show a difference in mass due to the air that has been added. Depending on the age level, you may also want to ask them if they think that the shrunken balloon will weigh less, more, or the same as the original balloon. They may be surprised to note that mass does not change in a closed system. Some may realize that if nothing is added or taken away, the result in mass is the same before and after cooling. If you can get a helium balloon, the result of the activity will be more dramatic but regular balloons react the same as far as size is concerned. Variables to investigate may include time in the cooler, size of the balloon, thickness of the rubber in the balloon, color of the balloon, and temperature differences, which can be accomplished by comparing freezer with refrigerator cooling. Many opportunities for controlling variables exist here and experience in talking through the experimental designs is also a valuable part of the activity. If you are using helium filled balloons, you can time the differences it takes for the balloon to rise from the floor to the ceiling. For this you would need a stopwatch. And don't forget to have the children write in their science notebooks!

I recommend your reading Bill Robertson's *Science and Children* article entitled, "Why Does Air Expand When You Heat It and Why Does Hot Air Rise?"

Latex can be a serious allergen, so it would be prudent to send a note home before this lesson to confirm all students can handle the balloons safely.

Using the Story With Grades 5–8

Many of the same kinds of questions will probably arise from the older children. The fact that the balloon reacts so readily to temperature gives fast feedback for experiments. These children need a great deal of work with talking science and designing experiments around gas volume and temperature. If they are capable of measuring the circumference of balloons before and after chilling, graphing of their results is a must. Some teachers have had success in attaching a strip of paper around the diameter of the balloon. When cooled, the paper might fall off the balloon or if heated, the paper might tear if the balloon stretches enough. The graph could match time in the freezer and circumference of the balloon (the paper or string). Also, if there is a thermometer in both the freezer and the refrigerator, you can graph temperature with circumference. Remember also the option of warming the balloon further to measure differences. Once again, I recommend your reading Bill Robertson's *Science and Children* article entitled, "Why Does Air Expand When You Heat It and Why Does Hot Air Rise?"

Now comes the question of floating in the atmosphere and overcoming the force of gravity with an upward force. Density is a difficult concept for many students to understand, mainly because they have to keep in mind two properties of a substance at once. These are volume and mass, not only of the object in question but also of the medium in which they are floating or sinking. Help them think of the atmosphere as a "liquid" in which the balloon floats. Its mass/volume ratio is less than that of an equal amount of room air, by volume, when it floats. When its mass/volume ratio becomes more than an equal amount of air by volume, it does not float. This is because the volume decreases due to the reduction in temperature or the natural loss of gas over time. You can feel the resisting force when you push down on a helium-filled balloon. It feels the same as pushing a hollow ball under water. This kinesthetic addition to learning can be powerful for many students. Even though the water's density makes this upward force greater than that of air, the feeling is so similar that most students get the point.

You might also be interested in giving your students a probe ("Comparing

Cubes" or "Floating High or Low") from *Uncovering Student Ideas in Science* (vol. 2) (Keeley, Eberle, and Tugel 2007). Either or both probes will give you a good idea about where your students are in their understanding of density.

Your students might also be interested in inquiring how much mass a balloon can lift off the ground and how the balloon's change in volume relates to this ability. This is a fairly indirect way of looking at the balloon's volume but comparing the heated balloon's or room temperature balloon's lifting power to the cooled balloon's lifting power can be done and graphed easily.

related NSTa press books and JOurnal articles

Burns, J. 2007. Bubbles on a soda can: A demonstration of Charles Law. *Science Scope* 30 (5): 60–64.

Driver, R., A. Squires, P. Rushworth, and V. Wood-Robinson. 1994. *Making sense of secondary science: Research into children's ideas.* London and New York: Routledge Falmer.

Keeley, P. 2005. *Science curriculum topic study: Bridging the gap between standards and practice.* Thousand Oaks, CA: Corwin Press.

Keeley, P., F. Eberle, and L. Farrin. 2005. *Uncovering student ideas in science: 25 formative assessment probes* (vol. 1). Arlington, VA: NSTA Press.

Keeley, P., F. Eberle, and J. Tugel. 2007. *Uncovering student ideas in science: 25 more formative assessment probes* (vol. 2). Arlington, VA: NSTA Press.

Robertson, B. 2006. Why does air expand when you heat it and why does hot air rise? *Science and Children* 44 (1): 60–62.

references

American Association for the Advancement of Science (AAAS). 1993 *Benchmarks for science literacy.* New York: Oxford University Press.

Keeley, P., F. Eberle, and J. Tugel. 2007. *Uncovering student ideas in science: 25 more formative assessment probes* (vol. 2). Arlington, VA: NSTA Press.

Lamorisse, A. 1956. *Le Ballon Rouge* (The Red Balloon) Films Montsourise.

National Research Council (NRC). 1996. *National science education standards.* Washington, DC: National Academy Press.

Robertson, B. 2006. Why does air expand when you heat it and why does hot air rise? *Science and Children* 44(1): 60–62.

CHAPTER 15

BOCCE, ANYONE?

L eo loved to play bocce, a game that has been popular for over 7,000 years. It is said that the Egyptians played it using polished round stones. Leo had a lovely, flat, green lawn in back of his house and the whole family played at least several times a week. The game is played with a set of four balls, or *bocce*, which are rolled toward a smaller ball called the *pallino*. Whichever player has a bocce that is closest to the pallino, scores points.

There are of course, rules for playing and scoring. The bocce balls are about 4½ inches (11.4 cm) in diameter and weigh about 3 pounds (1.26 kg). The pallino is only 1¾ inches (4.5 cm) in diameter. The pallino is first thrown from a line on one end of the bocce field and the players then roll their bocce from the same line to get as close as they can to it. At the beginning of each round the pallino is thrown and ends up in different places for each round.

Leo had a best friend named Paul and Paul would have liked to play too but there was a problem. Paul had special needs because he was in a wheelchair and had limited use of his hands as well as his legs. Leo wanted to play bocce with Paul but Paul was unable to roll the ball. Both boys thought and thought about how they could play bocce together because they spent hours together every day after school and on weekends.

One day when Leo was out practicing his bocce, they had an idea. What if, instead of rolling the bocce by hand, he rolled the ball down a ramp? Could they aim the ramp and do something to the ramp so that the bocce balls would roll different distances? Would it work? Only one way to find out, so they found a plywood board in the garage and got some bricks to prop it up and tried releasing the bocce from the top of the board.

"I could do that," Paul thought, " 'cause I can reach the top of the board and let the ball roll toward the pallino." They agreed on a rule that they had to release the ball from the top of the board (they would now officially call it a ramp) and not push it but just let it roll out onto the lawn. They would both use the ramp in the same way. If it became necessary, Leo would follow Paul's directions on moving the ramp up or down or to one side or the other.

But now they had another problem. Neither of them had much experience with ramps and they had to figure out how to aim it and how to get the ball to go as far as they wanted it to go. And then, to make matters even more complicated, Paul's cousin Amy decided to get Paul some bocce balls of his own and they were sure that Paul's weighed more than Leo's. Naturally, Paul wanted to use his own. Would that make a difference? Only way to find out was to try, and so they did. They solved their problems and had many hours of bocce together and both of them got so good that Paul and Leo were about even in games won. I wonder what they found out and how they got the bocce balls to go just where they wanted them to go?

BackGround

Purpose

Rolling objects are always fascinating for children. This story gives children an opportunity to find patterns in the process of rolling objects down ramps. Shades of Galileo! Since he was one of the first to actually do investigations by what "natural philosophers" of his day would have called "playing," he opened a new era in science investigations.

Related Concepts

- force
- kinetic energy
- gravity
- ramps (simple machines)
- velocity
- friction
- potential energy
- work
- momentum
- speed
- acceleration
- inertia

Don't Be Surprised

The physics of motion is beset with rules often described as, "under ideal conditions." Well, in the real world it is usually impossible to create ideal conditions and so we have to be a little circumspect when it comes to recreating the results of ideal laws. Yet, we still are able to revisit many of the laws of motion and draw some conclusions based on these laws developed by Sir Isaac Newton in the 17th century. Many of your students will believe the common misconception that heavy objects travel further than light objects when rolled down a ramp. On some surfaces (after they leave the ramp) they do, if the surface is smooth and provides little friction. They may also believe that heavier balls travel faster down a ramp than lighter balls and therefore reach the end of the ramp first, which is not true. This follows the common misconception that if two objects of different masses are dropped (in the absence of air resistance differences) the more massive one will strike the ground first.

The balls arrive at the same time if released at the same time. But don't give it away to the kids before they have a chance to figure it out for themselves by experimenting with objects! The boys in the story, and your students, are in for a surprise when they begin rolling objects down a ramp. There are so many questions that will be raised for them to test that they could be busy for some time.

Content Background

Isaac Newton (1642–1727) said that an object will continue to do whatever it is doing unless it is acted on by something and that something we call a *force*. Actually, what he really said was that "Every body continues in its state of rest, or of uniform motion in a straight line, unless it is compelled to change that state by forces impressed upon it." But the first statement is easier to remember. It is known as Newton's first law of motion or sometimes as the *law of inertia*. Inertia is the property of all objects that causes the object to resist change. The amount of inertia in any object is dependent on its mass. The more mass an object has, the more difficult it is to start it in motion, change its direction, or stop it from moving. Whether an object is standing still or moving at a high rate of speed, only a force will change its position or its motion. A lot of what the object does depends upon its position. If you are holding a ball in your hand and release it, the ball and the earth are attracted to each other by the force of gravity and since the earth is so much more massive, the ball does the falling toward the center of the earth. This is something we have all experienced since the days when we would throw our strained carrots out of the high chair just to see them hit the floor. Newton was clever enough to work out the mathematics of it and form general rules, defining forces and how they work. Forces are pushes and pulls, kicks, blows, punches, etc, some working through direct contact and others through a distance, without touching. Kicking a soccer ball is an example of direct contact and gravity and magnetism are examples of non touching forces acting through a distance. For this reason students may believe that force and energy are synonymous.

Many people, including a majority of children, believe that after an object is put into motion by a force, such as throwing a ball into the air, a force needs to continue acting on the object to keep it moving. This is a common misconception. Physicists like to work with ideas that can be quantified and so like to use the term momentum. Actually once an object is in motion it has momentum which is related to its mass and its velocity. An object with more mass or more velocity will have more momentum. Think about the difference between stopping a moving locomotive and a moving tennis ball if both are travelling at the same speed. Also consider a small bullet travelling at a high rate of speed. Since both mass and velocity (speed in a direction) are related here, a small bullet going at a tremendous speed has a great deal of momentum and can cause a great deal of damage to anything that stops its motion. You may have felt the sting when you caught a swiftly thrown ball. The mass was small but the velocity was large, thus the pain.

So what is the difference between inertia and momentum you may be asking. Well, inertia is mainly determined by the mass of the object, which in turn explains an object's resistance to change. More mass, more resistance. Momentum is this mass in motion in a specific direction and thus is defined as mass x velocity. For example, if someone kicks a soccer ball, the ball has a velocity and a mass. The goalie feels this momentum when she makes a save. The soccer ball however never changes its mass throughout the episode. The momentum was the only thing that changed when the ball was caught or deflected.

Balls placed at the top of a ramp will have the force of gravity pulling on them straight down which will cause them to move down the ramp. But another force is usually also at work, friction. There is friction from the air they pass through and also from the surface of the ramp itself. The amount of this friction will depend on the smoothness of the balls and the smoothness of the ramp itself.

There are also two types of energy at work in the implications of this story, potential energy and kinetic energy. Potential energy describes the energy that exists in the balls because of their position and due to the fact that they had been moved to the top of the ramp against the force of gravity. This endowed them with the potential to do work. This energy was transformed into kinetic energy, the energy of motion, as they move down the ramp.

But physics is based on ideal laws and they state that in an ideal situation, bocce balls should travel the same distance once they leave the ramp regardless of mass. (Friction is a force because it is capable of altering motion). In the classroom, children can compare the different results by rolling two solid balls of different masses down a ramp that empties out onto either a carpet or a slippery floor surface. The heavier ball will experience more friction on a carpet and the two balls should roll almost the same distance before stopping. However, when the balls leaves the ramp onto a slippery surface such as a linoleum, tile, or wooden floor there will be less friction and the more massive ball will probably travel further. Friction is less on a slippery surface than on a carpeted surface. This difference is actually a way to show the effect of friction and how it can affect the behavior of rolling or sliding objects.

Galileo first experimented with rolling objects on ramps in the 16th and 17th century because it helped him to explain what happens to falling objects. It turned out that falling objects and rolling objects behave the same and rolling balls down ramps allowed Galileo to have more control over the speed of the balls so that he could measure their motion more easily. Both dropped and rolled balls are affected by the force of gravity in a similar way and move from a higher to a lower position, following the same laws of gravity that Newton later explained.

I cannot possibly explain the whole of the physics of motion here. If you want to really find a good source on this topic, I suggest that you obtain copies of Bill Robertson's books, *Force and Motion* and *Energy*, from his *Stop Faking It!* Series (2004, 2005) available from NSTA press. These books in the series will help you to become a more confident teacher of these topics.

Science Ideas from National Science Education Standards (NRC 1996)

K–4: Position and Motion of Objects
- The position of an object can be described by locating it relative to another object or the background.
- An object's motion can be described by tracing and measuring the position over time.
- The position and motion of objects can be changed by pushing or pulling. The size of the change is related to the strength of the push or pull.

5–8: Motion and Forces
- The motion of an object can be described by its position, direction of motion and speed. That motion can be measured and represented on a graph.

- An object that is not being subjected to a force will continue to move at a constant speed and in a straight line.
- If more than one force acts on an object along a straight line, then the forces will reinforce or cancel one another, depending on their direction and magnitude. Unbalanced forces will cause changes in the speed or direction of an object's motion.

related ideas from Benchmarks for Science Literacy (aaas 1993)

K–2: Motion
- Things move in many different ways, such as straight, zigzag, round and round, back and forth, and fast and slow.
- The way to change how something is moving is to give it a push or pull.

3–5: Motion
- Something that is moving may move steadily or change its direction. The greater the force, the greater the change in motion will be. The more massive an object is, the less effect a given force will have.
- How fast things move differs greatly. Some things are so slow that their journey takes a long time; others move too fast for people to even see them.

6–8: Motion
- In the absence of retarding forces such as friction, an object will keep its direction of motion and its speed. Whenever an object is seen to speed up, slow down, or change direction, it can be assumed than an unbalanced force is acting on it.

Using the Story With Grades K–4

As usual, after reading the story to the class, ask them what they already know about how far rolling objects will travel after going down a ramp, and record these on the "Best Thinking" chart. They will probably bring up the idea of rolling different weights of balls before you need to suggest it. It is important to use two balls that differ only in mass. A good example would be a metal ball and a wooden or glass marble with the same diameter. With young children it is a particularly great opportunity to talk about fair investigations and to help them to identify and control the many variables involved. Some teachers find it useful to demonstrate the "wrong" methods to the children and ask them if what she is doing is fair. For example, if you push one ball and release the other or let one go before the other the children will immediately cry "foul." The height of the ramp or length of the

ramp must be controlled and then questions should pop up about what differences the height or angle of the ramp might cause. If you have access to the teachers' manual of the unit "Balls and Ramps," from the *Insights Program*, published by Kendall/Hunt, you might want to read it for some insight into what the children might suggest trying. Lessons 11 through 13 are particularly pertinent to this story. The unit as written is designed for first grade. The extent to which you are willing to take the children's questions and the curiosity of the children themselves will dictate how long you continue on this journey into the physics of motion. Remember to include time for recording their findings in their science notebooks and plenty of time for discussion of their activities and results. The vocabulary you decide to include will again depend on the class' willingness to learn and use new words. Introducing the vocabulary in the context of the activity will help the children make the connection between word and context.

I suggest that you read the next section for your own benefit so that you can see where the concept is going over the years. It will help you understand more about the physics of motion even though you will probably not use the ideas directly with your students at this time.

Using the Story With Grades 5–8

I suggest you read the section above about using the story with grades K–4. After reading the story, ask the class to pair up and share with their partner what they think the boys will have to do to make the bocce go where they want them to go. Record the results of these conversations on the "Best Thinking" chart and if possible turn them into questions. It is more likely that the older children will scoff at the boys' naiveté but you should ask them to provide some examples from their experience or some evidence to support their opinions. The combination of the pair-share activity and the recording of their ideas should provide enough doubt to merit some experimental design to prove their points. The main points addressed by the story are inertia forces and momentum. You may want to find out what forces they think are acting on the balls at various points down the ramp. Some students will identify gravity pulling the ball downward and friction where the ball meets the ramp or even friction from the air. Most will think that at the bottom of the ramp a force is still "in" the ball. This is a common misconception, even among adults. But, as you may know, at this point, the only force acting on the rolling ball is friction which now begins to change the motion of the ball and bring it to a halt. To paraphrase Newton, an object only changes its motion (or lack of it) when a force affects it. What the ball has at the bottom of the ramp is momentum, a word coined to account for the continued motion of the ball as it spends its allotment of kinetic energy as it battles friction which tries to slow it down.

Students know that it is harder to stop a moving bowling ball than it is to stop a moving tennis ball. They also know that it is harder to push a bowling ball into motion than it is a tennis ball. Physicists call this property of an object inertia. Inertia is the tendency of an object to keep on doing what it is doing, sitting on a couch or moving at 1000 miles per hour. This brings us to the famous equation, $F = ma$, where, F = force, m = mass, and a = acceleration. Acceleration is defined as any change of motion or direction. Thus, slowing down, to a physicist, is as much acceleration as going faster. Such is the confusing language of science and the even more confusing everyday language, where drivers call the gas pedal an accelerator which makes our cars go faster. Acceleration can also mean changing direction so when you turn on a curve, you are accelerating!

But let's go back to the $F = ma$ equation. If you make a simple algebraic change in the equation by dividing both sides by m, you find that $a = F/m$ or in other words the amount of acceleration a moving object has, is directly proportional to the force applied and inversely proportional to the mass of the object. Plainly stated, this means that the acceleration of an object increases if you apply a bigger push and decreases if you use the same amount of push on a heavier object. This explains the bowling ball/tennis ball phenomenon mentioned above.

Again, it is best to use two balls of different mass but of the same diameter. When the balls reach the end of the ramp, the heavier ball will have more momentum and by the same token it will be subject to more friction once it touches the floor it rolls upon. The lighter ball will have less momentum but will be subject to less friction once it touches the floor. The harder the ball presses on the floor, the more friction can be expected. But, on a carpeted floor, the friction will be more pronounced than on a slick floor due to the rougher, thicker pile of the carpet. The heavier ball will experience more friction due to its greater mass and the lighter ball, less due to its lesser mass. Thus the balls should go about the same distance, once leaving the ramp. On the smoother surface, like a slippery floor, the amount of frictional force is less effective and the more massive ball with its greater momentum will travel further than the lighter ball, despite Newton's "ideal law of physics." Paul and Leo will have to consider these ideas when they adjust the ramp to control the bocce and consider the frictional function of the grass.

Basically, what has happened here is that you have allowed the students to voice their preconceptions about moving and rolling objects; you then help them to design experiments to test these theories; they obtained their results and discussed them as a class; you explained the ideas of forces from the point of view of the physicist; they worked together to integrate their results with Newton's laws of motion and then tried to apply their new understanding by manipulating the several variables. More potential energy is added to the balls by increasing the height and angle of the ramp, since you must raise the balls higher. Different frictional forces are observed by trying different surfaces at the base of the ramp. The students have tested hypotheses, gained information about physical laws from the teacher and then accommodated their prior thinking to new situations using the ideas gained through both learning about the laws and evaluating them through experimentation.

Students may notice that the heavier and lighter balls both reach the end of the ramp at the same time and this may confuse them. They may even ignore the "ties" and concentrate on the situations where one ball does reach the end of the ramp slightly before the other. You must make them consider the ties as data. Students at any age may consider this acitivity as a race and concentrate on the "winner" and ignore the fact that the ties are data that tell them that there really is no winner. This means of course that many trials, perhaps ten, must be run so that data can be accumulated for analysis.

One can only conclude that the balls are caused to move, equally down the ramp by the force of gravity regardless of their mass. This has been shown over and over again by dropping two balls of different masses and noticing that they hit the floor at the same time. Try it and you will see. How can this be? I prefer to explain it in terms of inertia. The heavier ball resists the force of gravity more than the lighter ball because it has more inertia or resistance to moving. In essence, they balance out and reach the floor at the same time. It is actually more complicated than that but at this grade level it should be enough to leave the students pondering this strange but universal phenomenon. They should in the meantime have gained a much better understanding of the phenomenon of motion and forces.

An added activity might be to have the children invent games using balls and ramps, perhaps providing targets at which to aim the balls. They may think of others but it will give them a chance to apply their knowledge in their own ways.

related NSTA Press Books and Journal Articles

Adams, B. 2007. Energy in motion. *Science and Children* 44 (7) : 30–35.

Education Development Center. Balls and ramps. *Insights.* Kendall/Hunt: Dubuque, IA.

Keeley, P. 2005. *Science curriculum topic study: Bridging the gap between standards and practice.* Thousand Oaks, CA: Corwin Press.

Keeley, P., F. Eberle, and L. Farrin. 2005. *Uncovering student ideas in science: 25 formative assessment probes* (vol. 1). Arlington, VA: NSTA Press.

Keeley, P., F. Eberle, and J. Tugel. 2007. *Uncovering student ideas in science: 25 more formative assessment probes* (vol. 2). Arlington, VA: NSTA Press.

King, K. 2005. Making sense of motion. *Science Scope* 28 (6): 22–26

McCarthy, D. 2005. Newton's first law: A learning cycle approach. *Science Scope.* 28 (5): 46–49.

Robertson, W. C. 2002. *Energy: Stop faking it! Finally understanding science so you can teach it.* Arlington, VA: NSTA Press.

Robertson. W. C. 2002. *Force and motion: Stop faking it! Finally understanding science so you can teach it.* Arlington, VA: NSTA Press.

Robertson, W. C. 2007. What exactly is energy? *Science and Children* 44 (7): 62–63.

Science on Display. 2000. Roller coasters-Thrilling physics. *Science Scope.* 24 (1): 56–57.

Stroup, D. 2003. Balloons and Newton's Third Law. *Science Scope.* (Feb): 54.

Van Hook, S., and T. Hoziak-Clark. 2007. Spring into energy. *Science and Children* 44 (7): 21–25.

references

American Association for the Advancement of Science (AAAS). 1993. *Benchmarks for science literacy.* New York: Oxford University Press.

National Research Council (NRC). 1996. *National science education standards.* Washington, DC: National Academy Press.

Robertson, W. C. 2002. *Energy: Stop faking it! Finally understanding science so you can teach it.* Arlington, VA: NSTA Press.

Robertson. W. C. 2002. *Force and motion: Stop faking it! Finally understanding science so you can teach it.* Arlington, VA: NSTA Press.

CHAPTER 16
GRANDFATHER'S CLOCK

It was tall and skinny. Once it had been carried through the doors between the porch and the living room, it sat almost wedged between the floor and ceiling. It had a lovely face and delicate hands. In a way, it looked almost human and not a piece of furniture. The word beautiful came to Mary's mind. Her parents called it a grandfather's clock but her grandparents had not owned it as far as she knew. It had come to them from an aunt of her dad's who had died recently and willed the clock to them. Mary's

parents were quite excited about it—something about its being 200 years old and in the family for a long time and other stuff. Grownups seemed to think old things were really cool. Mary couldn't quite figure out why old things were cooler than brand new things, but whatever! The grandfather's clock was now in a place of honor, sitting against the wall and looking really big in their small house.

The clock was made of dark wood with a long narrow window in front. This window could be opened and inside there was a kind of metal pole that hung down from somewhere near the top of the clock. You could touch the pole. It had a brass dish about the size of a small saucer attached to it at the very bottom end. Mary's parents called the pole thing a pendulum. When you pulled the pendulum to one side and let it go, it kept swinging back and forth and the clock part up top made tick-tock noises. If it went long enough, you could see the hands on the face of the clock move. You also had to wind the clock with a key about once a week so the pendulum would go on swinging and the hands would go on moving. The hands of course told the time the old fashioned way, not like the neat digital face they had on other clocks. Mary guessed that the clock was pretty special to be working so well after 200 years of ticking and tocking. She had a digital alarm clock that hadn't lasted a year before it broke.

Two weeks passed and Mary made an observation. "Mom," she said, "the grandfather's clock is always running slower than the other clocks in the house."

"I noticed that too, Mary," replied her mother. "We have to move the hands ahead every day but it always runs slow. The next day we have to do it again and it never keeps good time. We looked for a button or switch to make it go faster but can't find any."

"The pendulum seems to make the clock go. Maybe it needs to swing faster," offered Mary. "But, how do we do that?"

"Maybe the dish on the bottom of the pendulum is too heavy," suggested Mom. "If it's too heavy, it could slow down the swing time."

"Or the pendulum swings too far from side to side—it takes too long to make a swing. If we could make it take shorter swings, it would go faster."

Mary shared her problem with her teacher, Ms. Patel, the next day. "It's a beautiful old clock," complained Mary, "but it doesn't keep good time, so in a way, it's useless."

"Why don't you set the clock to go faster?" asked Ms. Patel.

"How? We can't find any switches or buttons!" replied Mary. "We think the long pole that comes down from the top has something to do with how fast the clock goes but we can't seem to make the pole change speed."

"That pole and the bob on the bottom is called a pendulum," Ms. Patel explained to the whole class. "They swing in regular patterns but we have to know more about them in order to change how they move.

"Let's make some pendulums out of string and washers," suggested Ms. Patel. "We can test these and see if we can find ways to speed them up or slow them down. So, for a start," she said as she drew the pendulum on the board, "What parts of the pendulum can we change? And how can we find out if changing these parts is what makes a difference in how fast they swing?"

Later that week, after experimenting with the pendulums in class, Mary went home and fixed the clock. Now it keeps perfect time but if it doesn't someday, Mary and her family know just how to fix it. It really is simple—when you know how.

Background

Purpose

The main purpose of studying the pendulum in this story is to provide a vehicle for finding and sorting out variables and designing a study for discovering the variable that controls the period (the time for a back and forth swing) of the pendulum. The physics of the pendulum is much too sophisticated for young children and will wait for later years. On the other hand, it will come as a surprise to most students, and possibly to adults, that the only variable that makes a difference in the period of the pendulum is the length of the pendulum. The period is defined as the time it takes for the pendulum to make one complete swing, forth and back.

If possible obtain the October 2006 issue of *Science and Children* and read the featured article "Inquiry on Board." This article by Helen Buttemer shows how, using easily constructed visual aids, you can visually guide the planning, conducting, and analyzing of experiments such as the one required in this story. Dr. Buttemer makes the set up and design of an experiment clear to students of all ages by putting variables on sticky notes and moving them through the design process so that students can participate in the process and see the results. It will make a difference in your students understanding of experimental design. I cannot recommend it highly enough.

Related Concepts

- periodic motion
- time
- variables
- fair tests
- analysis
- period of the pendulum
- hypothesis
- controls experiment
- data
- conclusions

Don't Be Surprised

This activity will bring out many preconceptions including (1) the weight of the pendulum affects the period and (2) the size of the swing affects the period. Another outcome of the activities may be the discovery that the pendulum may be used as a timing device. It seems so counterintuitive that the weight does not affect the period that your students may not believe their own data. The investigation may have to be done as a demonstration and any deviation may be an excuse for them to challenge the result. Their expectation will be that the further the pendulum swings or the heavier the pendulum bob is, the shorter the period.

Content Background

Mary's solution to taming the unruly grandfather's clock is a very simple one. The pendulum must be shorter in order to swing more often in a given period of time. Actually the word "period" is an important one here since the time taken for the pendulum to make one swing forward and back to its original position is called its period.

When children are ready for terminology they may be introduced to the terms "independent or manipulated variable" (the variable that is modified, e.g. the length of pendulum, the weight of the bob, or the amplitude of the swing). The "dependent or observed variable" is the variable that is measured for possible change. In this case it is the period of the pendulum. Children in grades 5–8 are ready for this kind of terminology.

The only adjustment needed to lessen the period is shortening the pendulum. In a clock, the pendulum bob, the weight at the end of the pendulum, is raised to shorten the period or lowered to increase the period. In effect, this adjustment changes the center of gravity of the entire system having the same effect as changing the length of the rod. With the shortening of the pendulum, the period is also shortened and the pendulum system takes less time to swing to and fro. Since the pendulum is attached to the clock gears, the more swings in a given time period causes the gears to move more quickly and the hands of the clock to move more rapidly—therefore we say that the clock speeds up. The lowering of the bob would have the opposite effect, slowing down the mechanism and the clock. The pendulum length is actually measured from the pivot point to the center of mass of the pendulum. If one is using washers for a bob, the center of mass is probably in the center of the washer, or close enough to this point for all practical purposes.

The pendulum is one example of a system that exhibits what we call periodic motion. Periodic motion simply means that the motion of objects in a system moves in a predictable way, which is usually cyclical in nature. Other examples would be a vibrating object such as a guitar string or tuning fork, the Moon's motion around the Earth, the Earth's motion around the Sun, or the Earth's rotation on its axis. Therefore, learning about periodic motion has implication for many natural phenomena. It is a big idea or conceptual scheme, which can be used in many situations to help us understand models, which in turn explain the world around us. In the story "Where are the Acorns?" the movement of shadows during the day or over the seasons is used as an indicator of what appears to be the periodic motion of the sun as it appears to move across the daytime sky from dawn to sunset. Constellations exhibit periodic motion in the northern and southern hemispheres. We have constellations that only appear in the winter and others that are only seen in the summer. The constellations appear to move in predictable patterns across the sky during the night due to the rotation of the earth. Planets such as Venus and Mars move predictably among the stars because they have their own periodic motion around the sun. One of the most important aspects of periodicity is that it helps us to predict happenings and to build models of the universe, which in turn help us to explain how things work.

It might be important here to reemphasize the term system. A system is a collection of interconnected parts (or objects) that interact with each other. In many animal bodies we have organs that make up digestive systems, circulatory systems, nervous systems, etc. In plants there are tissues that constitute water conducting systems, leaves, and roots. In the universe, we have solar systems, intergalactic systems. In nature, we have ecosystems and in weather we have the atmosphere. They all have in common the fact that the system is a whole made up of parts and that these systems behave according to certain rules. One most important rule is that if you change one part of the system, the entire system responds and changes

in some way. For example, if, in an ecosystem, a plant or animal is removed, the entire system is changed to accommodate its removal. If a predator is removed, its prey will increase in number and perhaps eat more vegetation, which in turn will affect the food supply for other animals. You will find that looking at nature as a series of systems can be very useful.

From the story line, it becomes apparent that the students need to work with pendulums and find out what can be done to the pendulum system to change the number of swings the pendulum makes in any given time period or the period of the pendulum. If you as the teacher do this activity before trying it with the students, you will want to figure out how you will identify and test the variables involved. From the story, the clues can be identified from the conversation between Mary and her mother. Identified were the length of the pendulum, the weight on the pendulum bob, and the distance the pendulum swings. In physics, this latter would be called the amplitude of the swing. What we now have is a set of variables that have to be tested against the problem from the story of how to change the pendulum's period. The period is usually defined as the time it takes for the pendulum to swing from one side and back to that side again— i.e. back and forth. Since the back and forth swing of the clock's pendulum has been tentatively identified as the keeper of the time on the clock, the number of swings in any given time period must be changed by modifying the pendulum system. A system is defined as a group of objects interacting with each other. In this case, the system includes the pendulum bob and the connecting rod. When you make a pendulum, I suggest that you use a tongue depressor, available from your doctor's office or from most pharmacies, a thin string about 50 cm long, a paper clip and some washers, available from your workshop or a local hardware store. Figure 16.1 shows the pendulum system and its parts.

You will notice that the tongue depressor has been cut so that there is a split running lengthwise for about 2–3 cm. The string slides into this slot and it can be pulled up and down to change the length of the string easily. The clip is bent to make a hook so that the washers can be added and subtracted easily and the clip is tied to the other end of the string. The tongue depressor is then taped to the desk or table, sticking out far enough so that the string does not rub against the table and swings freely.

Now that you have the pendulum you must decide how each of the variables relates to the period of the pendulum. This of course is the purpose of the inquiry and will result in the answer for Mary as to how to

Figure 16.1
The pendulum system.

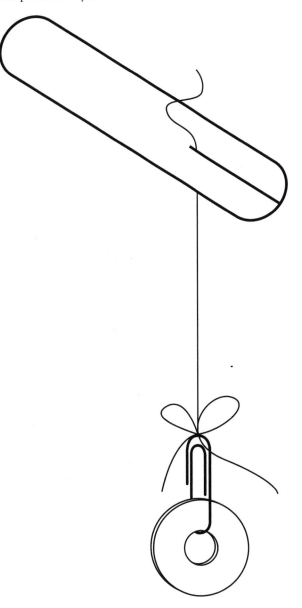

"set" her clock. You must find a way to test each of the variables while keeping the others unchanged. Let us suppose that you are going to test the effect of the weight of the bob. Your hypothesis would be either, "The weight of the bob will change the period of the pendulum" or "The weight of the bob will not change the period of the pendulum." This means that the length of the string and the size of the swing must be kept constant while you are testing the effect of the weight of the bob. You might decide to let the pendulum swing for 15 seconds and see how many periods the pendulum makes. You will probably want to repeat your experiment five or more times to be sure that any error you might make would be nullified. You could take the average of the five trials and throw out any data that were exceptionally off track. Next you would add a washer or two and repeat the experiment. Your result might be surprising! There would be no difference, no matter how many washers you added. Your conclusion would be that the mass of the bob does not effect the period of the pendulum. Your evidence would be in your data and the analysis of those data would bear out your conclusion.

Next you might try to see if the amplitude of the swing has any effect. Again you state your hypothesis. You keep the number of washers and the length of the string constant and try different spots from which to release the bob. Again you try each spot five times and record your results. Surprise again? No difference in the period regardless of where you release the bob. Logically, the pendulum must swing faster in order to make a longer round trip in the same amount of time. That leaves only one variable left to try, the length of string. You state your hypothesis regarding the length of string and period change and then do the experiment using the same design for acquiring data. This time, you see some differences. The shorter the string, the more swings you count in 15 seconds. The longer the string, the fewer swings you get in 15 seconds. Your conclusion would be that the length of the string affects the period of the pendulum. Your data back up your conclusion. You can now complete the story and solve Mary's problem. Actually, the pendulums of grandfathers' clocks do not have a way of changing the length of the rod but you can shorten or lengthen the pendulum system by raising or lowering the bob which in essence does the same thing as changing the length of the pendulum since physicists have found that the real length of the pendulum is measured from the pivot point to the center of the bob. Looking back, you have managed to isolate the variables in the system and found a way to test each of the variables individually while keeping the other variables constant. The data were analyzed and conclusions made using the data to corroborate the conclusions. The new understanding was then applied to the situation in the story, which amounts to an application of learning to a new situation. All steps of the inquiry process have been covered. See Chapter One again to review the essentials of the inquiry process for students.

related ideas from national science education standards (nrc 1996)

K–4: Abilities Necessary to Do Scientific Inquiry

- Ask a question about objects, organisms and events in the environment.
- Plan and conduct a simple investigation.
- Employ simple equipment and tools to gather data and extend the senses.
- Use data to construct a reasonable explanation.
- Communicate investigations and explanations.

5–8: Abilities Necessary to Do Scientific Inquiry

- Identify questions that can be answered through scientific investigations.
- Design and conduct a scientific investigation.
- Use appropriate tools and techniques to gather, analyze, and interpret data.
- Think critically and logically to make the relationships between evidence and explanations.

related ideas from Benchmarks for science literacy (aaas 1993)

K–2: Scientific inquiry

- People can often learn about things around them by just observing those things carefully, but sometimes they can learn more by doing something to the things and noting what happens.
- Describing things as accurately as possible is important in science because it enables people to compare their observations with those of others.
- When people give different descriptions of the same thing, it is usually a good idea to make some fresh observations instead of just arguing about who is right.

3–5: Scientific Inquiry

- Results of scientific investigations are seldom exactly the same, but if

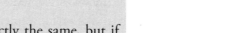

the differences are large, it is important to try to figure out why. One reason for following directions carefully and for keeping records of one's work is to provide information on what might have caused the differences.

- Scientists do not pay much attention to claims about how something they know about works unless the claims are backed up with evidence that can be confirmed with a logical argument.

6–8: Scientific Inquiry

- If more than one variable changes at the same time in an experiment, the outcome of the experiment may not be clearly attributable to any on of the variables. It may not always be possible to prevent outside variables from influencing the outcome of an investigation but collaboration among investigators can often lead to research designs that are able to deal with such situations.

Using the Story With Grades K–4

Constructing and testing the pendulums is the main activity in following up on this story. Ms. Patel suggests to the class that they should make and test pendulums to help Mary solve her problem, which is to make the clock tell the correct time. The suggestions for making simple pendulums are given in the content background section above.

We refer you to the *National Science Education Standards* essay on Pendulums on pgs 146–147 for an excellent look at how one teacher uses the task.

This story however, leads into solving the problem of how to fix the clock. Mary needs to find a way to speed the clock up since it loses minutes each day. She has deduced that the pendulum has something to do with the accuracy of the clock and now must find a way to change the period of the pendulum.

Help the children to identify the variables listed in the story. The clues lie in the conversation between Mary and her mother. Both the distance of the swing and the weight of the bob are mentioned as possible problems. Help the children find the third variable, the length of the pendulum, by looking at the pendulums they have built and looking at how many variables could be changed. Once the three have been identified, the design of the experiment can begin. If you can obtain a copy of the *Science and Children* article "Inquiry on Board," the use of Inquiry Boards will help your students understand the use of variables and controls (Buttemer 2006).

Here is your opportunity to conduct a scientific discourse. The children have built the pendulum systems and need to talk about the variables, the fair tests they need to conduct, and agree on the amount of time to use for counting swings. Many will suggest a whole minute but you may be able to convince them after one trial that one minute is too long and that a shorter time period would be just as ac-

curate. You might want to talk with them about possible errors that can be made, e.g. counting, starting the counting at the same time as the release, and how many swings would constitute a real "difference." For example, if the numbers of washers are tripled and a difference of one swing is noticed, would that be enough of a difference to count? You will probably want to talk about how many trials are necessary to be sure you have good data. And of course, you may try to figure out how each of the trial data is going to be recorded. You could use a graphic organizer or worksheet if you feel your students need it. If they can be involved in the design of the sheet, you can avoid children filling in blanks without knowing why they are doing so. Much of this can be recorded in their science notebooks if you give them time to do so and remind them of the various things you have discussed.

My experience is that four students make up a good experimenting group for this activity. One will release the pendulum and say, "go," the second will count the swings, the third will read the clock and say "stop," and the fourth will record the data. When getting materials, the materials can be in different parts of the room and each member of the group can be assigned a part to be retrieved thus eliminating traffic problems.

Measuring can be a problem for younger children. If your students cannot use a ruler or tape yet, it might be a good time to teach them. Barring their readiness for such a task, you might have them measure from the bottom of the tongue depressor to the middle of the washer hole according to tapes or strings you have made up in advance. I suggest three different lengths to give reasonable data, but in a pinch, two lengths will make the point.

It helps if you have a second-hand clock on the wall or can obtain one and place it where everyone can see. With much younger children, you may have to be timekeeper and have the students do their experimenting in unison. You may want to have a student demonstrate the process and all students count swings just for practice.

Now you are ready for groups to actually experiment. If your students are very independent you can tell them to test all three variables at their leisure. Remind them to write in their science notebooks a hypothesis for each variable, including results, conclusions, and evidence. If your students need a bit of organization, tell them that the class is going to test, say, weight first and then complete that segment before going on to the next variable. Together you can discuss with the class that they need to state an hypothesis for each variable, record this in their science notebooks, run the tests, draw conclusions, and justify their conclusions on the basis of the data. You may be free, if you are not timekeeper, to rove among the groups and observe their work and help those groups who need some direction.

After all of the data are in and each group has come up with their conclusions, it is time to share as a class. The discourse here can be centered on their findings and how they can use the information they have garnered to see how Mary might have solved her problem. If there are discrepancies in the findings, you can invite the disagreeing parties to reperform their experiments with the class as judge. Usually, little mistakes are picked up and a consensus can be reached. Now they are ready to finish the story and some of their creative literacy can be used. You might instruct them to finish the story complete with data to substantiate the way Mary could fix her clock. This can go in their science notebooks or in another form you prefer. In conclusion, I would suggest that you go over their procedure with them so that they think about what they did and stress the vocabulary involved in problem solving and inquiry. You might even challenge them to provide evidence to show that they are able to build a pendulum that will measure 30 complete swings in one minute and thereby building a time piece.

Using the Story With Grades 5–8

I suggest that you read the background material for grades K–4 as well as this section since there are a great number of similarities in the procedure. Your students, being more sophisticated and able to work on their own more than the younger students, will usually give you more options and perhaps a bit more freedom to observe their experimenting, during which time you can assess their growth by watching and listening to their communication with others in their group. I suggest that you work with groups of four just as in the suggestions listed above. The materials and the pendulums would be identical to those used by the younger students. Your students will also be able to measure lengths with rulers and tapes and keep more sophisticated records in their science notebooks. You can tell them that scientists usually measure to the middle of the bob, which will be the middle of the hole in the washers you use. The procedure is basically the same as for younger students with modifications you feel are justified due to the difference in maturity. I have found however, that if older students have not been involved in inquiry before, they sometimes need just as much guidance as do the younger ones, at least for a while. They too have to be reminded about controlling variables and may be introduced to the terms independent or manipulated variable (the variable that is deliberately modified, e.g., the length of pendulum, the weight of the bob, or the amplitude of the swing). The dependent or responding variable is the variable that is measured for possible change, and the controlled variables—the variables that we intentionally keep the same so we can be sure that the manipulated variable alone is responsible of any change in the dependent variable. In this case it is the period of the pendulum that is the dependent or responding variable. Children in grades 5-8 are usually ready for this kind of terminology. It will also contribute to their ability to read literature about experiments with understanding.

You may want to use graphic organizers with your students if it seems necessary but be sure that they keep track of their work in their science notebooks so that they have a record of their thinking and their activity. They are now in a position to finish the story and talk about and write about how Mary fixed her clock to keep good time. If you are fortunate enough to have a small pendulum clock, the students can try out their solutions on the clock, e.g., make it go faster or slower. Barring this, find a musical metronome, which can do the same thing. I suggest that, as in the case of the younger students, you ask your students to construct a pendulum that keeps time at a given rate. This will offer you another chance at an assessment of their learning.

RELATED NSTA PRESS BOOKS AND JOURNAL ARTICLES

Buttemer, H. 2006. Inquiry on board. *Science and Children* 43 (2): 34–39.

Driver, R., A. Squires, P. Rushworth, and V. Wood-Robinson. 1994. *Making sense of secondary science: Research into children's ideas.* London and New York: Routledge Falmer.

Keeley, P. 2005. *Science curriculum topic study: Bridging the gap between standards and practice.* Thousand Oaks, CA: Corwin Press.

Keeley, P., F. Eberle, and L. Farrin. 2005. *Uncovering student ideas in science: 25 formative assessment probes* (vol. 1). Arlington, VA: NSTA Press.

Keeley, P., F. Eberle, and J. Tugel. 2007. *Uncovering student ideas in science: 25 more formative assessment probes* (vol. 2). Arlington, VA: NSTA Press.

references

American Association for the Advancement of Science (AAAS). 1993. *Benchmarks for science literacy.* New York: Oxford University Press.

National Research Council (NRC). 1996. *National science education standards.* Washington, DC: National Academy Press.

CHAPTER 17

THE NEIGHBORHOOD TELEPHONE SYSTEM

aurie lived next door to Maria. They were best friends and had been since kindergarten. Now, in the fourth grade, they seemed to spend more time together than ever. Every evening after supper they would be on the phone, yakking away about all sorts of things.

"Hey, you have been on the phone for an hour!" said Maria's dad. "I'd like to use the phone too."

"Right!" said her mom. "I'm expecting a call from Auntie Felicia tonight."

"But I'm taking to Laurie," begged Maria. Suddenly Maria had an idea. "Hey, why don't you and Laurie's parents get us our own phones; cell phones might be really nice? Then we wouldn't be on your phone all the time."

"Do you have any idea how much the monthly bills are?" said her dad. "For Pete's sake, you live right next door. You can practically talk to each other from your bedroom windows…." Suddenly he stopped. "That's it!" he cried. "You can talk to each other from your bedroom windows."

"Daaaad," Maria laughed, "everybody in the neighborhood would hear us shouting at each other from our windows!"

"No, no, no!" exclaimed Maria's dad. "You can use TCTS. Completely private and really, really, cool. And the price is perfect!"

"Okay, I give up, what is TCTS?" asked Maria.

"No mystery. It's a simple device, two tin cans connected by a string. Now can you guess what TCTS stands for?" asked her dad.

This all sounded interesting so Maria talked to Laurie the next day and they decided to give this idea a try. With a little help from Maria's mom and dad, they used two empty tomato cans connected by a long string knotted on the inside of the cans, so that it would not come out of the hole punched in the can. It looked like this.

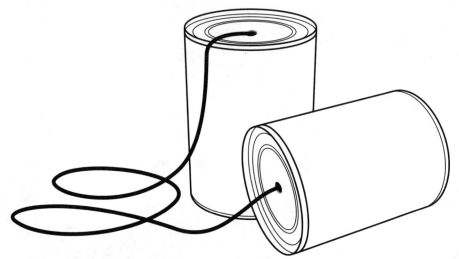

In no time at all they had the telephone system set up between the windows of their rooms and were ready to try it out. Laurie held her can up to her ear and Marie talked softly into the can on her side, hoping that her voice would travel along the string to Laurie. Nothing! Their mothers were waiting below and shouted up, "you have to have the string between the cans pulled tightly."

The girls pulled the string tight and soon they were talking to each other across the distance although the words were not always clear.

"Why does the string have to be tight?" shouted Laurie.

"Good question. Think about it a while and we'll talk," said Mom.

"What's so magic about the string?" asked the girls.

"Another good question!" said Mom. "Another question to think about."

"How can we make it clearer? Sometimes I can barely make out your words," asked Laurie.

"How about using bigger cans?" asked Maria. "Or maybe a plastic or paper cup instead?"

"Or, using bigger string, maybe?" replied Laurie.

"Or use something other than a string. Maybe a wire?" added Maria's mom. "Maybe the sound will travel better through a wire."

"Looks like we have some experimenting to do," said the girls.

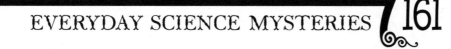

Background

Purpose

This story has a two-pronged purpose. One has to do with learning something about sound (science) and the other has to do with learning about using science to modify the things in the world to solve human problems (technology).

Few adults have not had the opportunity to use a "tin can" telephone (TCT) during his or her childhood. The goal of transmitting sound across a distance has been around for a long time. It is even rumored that Alexander Graham Bell, the inventor of the telephone, played and experimented with one as he was closing in on his invention that would change the world. Obviously Bell was trying to eliminate the string but the principles of vibration and transmission of sound waves were still the guiding principles. Bell found a way to transmit the vibrations electrically, eliminating the need for direct contact between the speakers. This story uses the TCT as a focus for inquiry into the transmission of sound waves along a medium and also provides an opportunity for kids to try their hand at improving a simple device so that it works better. Students will experiment with various parts of the TCT changing variables and trying to find the best combination for optimum transmission of their voices.

In this electronic age, it is probably difficult for children to imagine a time before cell phones, television, blackberries, palm pilots, and portable media systems. Yet, it is often exciting for children to backtrack and experience the earlier days before modern communication and information technology became a way of life. School curricula are full of demonstrations of sound transmission through solid and liquid media but here in the TCT story is an opportunity to investigate an old toy and find out what makes it tick. There is plenty of room for the science and technology aspects of the standards to be applied. Building a better mousetrap is usually exciting for students and here is one that gives instant feedback, and makes changing variables easy and fun. If you play with one before you take the idea to your students you will find that several variables make a difference in sound transmission. It will also help you to be prepared with different materials for students to use in their experimentation. You will also notice the inclusion of the technology standards in this background material so that you can see what types of technology standards as well as science standards can be met.

Related Concepts

- waves
- sound transmission
- energy
- technological design
- sound
- vibration
- energy transmission

Don't Be Surprised

Children may reject the use of nonmetallic objects to design the telephone since they usually think of sound coming from vibrating metals such as cymbals or strings. Children also think of sound as a substance that moves from the sender to the receiver. On the other hand, those who believe in sound emanating from vibrating objects may immediately connect the string or wire connecting the "cans" as picking up vibrations and transmitting sound.

Content Background

Sound waves, like all waves, are energy waves. All waves transmit energy. Sound waves emanate from vibrating objects. They travel through air or any other medium but can be distorted by other sounds or anything that can disrupt the medium through which the waves travel. Vibrations in the originator of the sound such as vocal cords, drum skins, objects falling on pavement, clapping hands, or a multitude of banging or clanging can generate sound waves which then travel through gas, liquid or solid but not through a vacuum. This is because they need to excite molecules in the medium so that they transfer the energy of the original sound to nearby molecules, which then transfer them on to others in the form of a sound wave. These waves are compression waves and might be visualized as lines on a bar code, pushing against each other in a uniform pattern so that the sound travels from one end to the other. You may remember a science teacher from your past placing an alarm clock in a vacuum jar, and removing the air from within it. If the clock was ringing, the sound stopped when the air was removed. There were no molecules of any sort to be excited by the energy generated by the alarm. This of course brings up the old philosophical quandary, "If a tree falls in a forest where no one is present, does it still make a sound?" Sound needs no ear to hear it. It occurs whether one hears it or not.

Sound waves can bounce off objects and appear to come from different directions. If you have been in a noisy public place, surrounded by hard, bare surfaces, you may remember how difficult it is to converse with people near you. Sounds from other conversations and other noise bounce off these surfaces and literally fill the room with their presence. If you have experienced an echo, the same principle applies except that the bouncing sound wave is more focused and not mixed with other sounds.

Sound waves can be amplified by electronic means or by acoustic devices such as megaphones. Guitars, violins, and other stringed instruments make use of an acoustic amplifier by designing a way for the vibrating string to set up vibrations in an attached or surrounding structure. This changes the volume of the sound you hear. In the TCT, the can or cup into which the child speaks vibrates according to the sound waves made by the speaker. These sound waves are transferred to the string or wire and transmitted through the medium to the other cup, which in turn vibrates in the same way and also amplifies the sound transmitted down the string to the listener. It may be an important clue for you to know that amplifiers usually have cones made of paper in them. Different materials vibrate according to their structure. You will find that metal cans are not the best amplifiers since the construction of the can will cause different frequencies to travel at different speeds in the metal and produce garbled sounds. Plastic cups may be used to see how they act as amplifiers.

An object can produce sounds of varying pitches, giving a higher or lower sound. This usually is accomplished by changing the speed of the vibrating object. If you are plucking a rubber band or a guitar string, you may make the pitch higher or lower by either stretching (higher) the vibrating strand or relaxing it (lowering). You may also use a thinner string (higher) or a thicker string (lower), which, respectively, makes the plucked string vibrate faster or slower.

There are other things that vibrate which are not so easy to see. Let's say someone drops keys on a tabletop. You hear the sound and from experience recognize the sound as keys hitting a tabletop. This is a combination of your brain's memory of past experiences and your ear's ability to capture the resulting sound wave and send the vibration to the brain through the auditory nerve. But I just said that all sound was caused by vibrations so what caused the sound wave and vibration? I didn't mention any strings or drum skins, just keys and a table. Here is the problem that escapes most adults and children. Both the table and the keys vibrate as the keys hit the table and set the sound wave energy in motion and straight to our ears and ultimately our brains. We live in a world of sound and most of us hearing folks have learned to identify the sound vibrations that enter our ears. It is a good thing too, since screeching tires, auto horns, and other alarms help us to avoid nasty confrontations with moving objects larger than we are.

Technology is an important aspect of science and technology education. In this story, there is an opportunity for children to see the aspects of problem solving and its relationship to design. The use of the term technology in the Standards is often confused with "instructional technology," which includes computers, digital microscopes, and other devices that help science teachers conduct their lessons. The difference is in goals. In the Standards, technology aims at giving children the opportunity to modify the environment to meet human needs. There are a series of five stages, which provide a framework for teachers to use in planning and assessing outcomes in technology. These five stages are:

- Stating the problem
- Designing an approach
- Implementing a solution
- Evaluating the solution
- Communicating the problem, design, and solution (NRC 1996, p. 137)

These stages are not to be construed as steps but as guidelines. Sometimes the objective will be to evaluate, for example, the relative properties of paper towels or shampoos. Other times they are guidelines to improving the mousetrap or in this case, the TCT. And at other times, the development of a specific invention or a device needed to solve a problem or challenge will be necessary.

related ideas from national science education standards (nrc 1996)

K–4: *Position and Motion of Objects*

- Sound is produced by vibrating objects. Changing the rate of vibration can vary the pitch of the sound.

5–8: *Transfer of Energy*

- Energy is a property of many substances and is associated with heat, light, electricity, mechanical motion, sound, nuclei, and the nature of a chemical. Energy is transferred in many ways.

K–4: *Abilities of Technological Design*

- Identify a simple problem
- In problem identification, children should develop the ability to explain a problem in their own words and identify a specific task and solution related to the problem.
- Propose a solution
- Students should make proposals to build something or get something to work better; they should be able to describe and communicate their ideas. Students should recognize that designing a solution might have constraints, such as cost, materials, time, space or safety.

5–8: *Abilities of Technological Design*

- Design a solution or product.
- Students should make and compare different proposals in the light of the criteria they have selected. They must consider constraints—such as time, trade-off s, and materials needed—and communicate ideas with drawings and simple models.
- Implement a proposed design.
- Students should organize materials and other resources, plan their work, make good use of group collaboration where appropriate, choose suitable tools and techniques, and work with appropriate measurement methods to ensure adequate accuracy.
- Evaluate completed technological designs or products.
- Students should use criteria relevant to the original purpose or need, consider a variety of factors that might affect acceptability and suitability for intended users and beneficiaries and develop measures of quality with respect to such criteria and factors; they should also suggest improvement and, for their own products, try proposal modification.

RELATED IDEAS FROM BENCHMARKS FOR SCIENCE LITERACY (AAAS 1993)

K–2: Motion

- Things that make sound vibrate.

6–8: Motion

- Something can be "seen" when light waves emitted or reflected by it enter the eye—just as something can be "heard" when waves from it enter the ear.
- Vibrations in materials set up wavelike disturbances that spread away from the source. Sound and earthquake waves are examples. These and other waves move at different speeds in different materials.

K–2: The Nature of Technology

- Tools are used to do things better or more easily and to do some things that could not otherwise be done at all. In technology, tools are used to observe, measure and make things.
- When trying to build something or to get something to work better, it usually helps to follow directions if there are any or to ask someone who has done it before for suggestions.
- People alone or in groups are always inventing new ways to solve problems and get work done. The tools and ways of doing things that people have invented affect all aspects of life.

K–2: Designs and Systems

- People can use objects and ways of doing things to solve problems.

3-5 Designs and Systems

- Even a good design may fail. Sometimes steps can be taken ahead of time to reduce the likelihood of failure, but it cannot be entirely eliminated.

6–8: Designs and Systems

- Design usually requires taking constraints into account. Some constraints, such as gravity or the properties of the materials to be used, are unavoidable.
- Technology cannot always provide successful solutions for problems or fulfill every human need.

3–5: The Nature of Technology

- Throughout all of history, people everywhere have invented and used tools. Most tools of today are different from those of the past but many are modifications of very ancient tools.
- Any invention is likely to lead to other inventions. Once an invention exists, people are likely to think up ways of using it that were never imagined at first.

Using the Story With Grades K–4

After reading the story, students should be asked to list their statements explaining why the TCT works. You will get a great many ideas of how sound gets from one person to another. It is really necessary that children have an idea of how sound travels from the vibrations set up in the cup, through the line, and is amplified in the receiving cup. List these on a "Best Thinking" chart for future referral. Next, try to elicit from the children their ideas about what kinds of things can be changed in the TCT in order to test what changes might get it to work better. You may also help them to realize that they need to decide what "better" means. Does louder make it better? Does hearing words more clearly make it better? Since the purpose in the story was to allow the girls to talk to each other, perhaps the latter is more important but the former can be a responding variable too, if the children so desire. They must be clear on what they are measuring and should keep notes and drawings in their science notebooks. Obviously, the activity will require working in pairs at a minimum since the TCTs must be far enough apart to test their efficiency.

Making the phones is a simple process but may need the help of an adult for safety's sake. First make sure that the cans are the same size, are open on one end, and that any jagged edges are either eliminated or covered over with heavy tape. A small hole should be made in the center of the intact end so that a string, wire, thread, or other medium can be pushed through the hole, knotted on the inside so that it will not slip back out and tested by pulling. Now that the cans are ready, the children can test them and see if they are able to understand each other. They will certainly hear some sounds although the exact words may not be clear. Thus comes the need to try different materials to see if the system can be improved. You are now into the technology standards as well as the science standards.

You may want to have on hand, larger cans, paper cups of varying sizes, plastic cups of varying sizes, wire, cotton twine, plastic cord, etc. The cord's length may also be a variable the children want to test but for starters you may want to suggest that four to five meters be standard for all trials. If the children forget to keep the strings taut, reread the part of the story that makes this point. With younger children it will probably be necessary to allow them to experiment with vibrating objects and make sounds so that they can see that the string must be free to vibrate. If they use rubber bands, help them to see that the bands must be tight in order to produce a sound. If they stretch balloons over cans like a drum skin, they can also see the amplification caused by the sound box. Many of the tried and true sound activities will be more meaningful once they are attached to the story. Finally the children will probably come to the conclusion that the larger paper cups and cotton twine will work the best but their results may vary. The most important thing is that they have a better understanding of how sound travels through various media and will have experienced the technology techniques involved in improving a device.

Using the Story With Grades 5–8

Once again I recommend that you read the suggestions given for grades K-4 before moving on to this section. Many of your students will own cell phones and will already have caused a problem in your classroom. They may have difficulty in understanding the relevance for improving this "low tech" toy. It helps to turn this story into a technology oriented task by asking them to become a toy company R & D (Research and Development) department given the task by the president or CEO of the company to produce the best product for sale to the public. In this case, you may want to develop with the help of the class a rubric with minimum standards set up that must be met. In other words, each group of students must develop a telephone that performs to standards set up by the entire class. Meeting these standards becomes the goal for those wishing to receive the highest grade and since they have been involved in setting the standards, they are involved in the evaluation of their product and their group's effort.

I have used a letter "written" by the company president giving the R & D group the challenge for producing a good toy. The letter should state that including the principles of how the toy works is important because written material describing these principles will be distributed along with the toy. They might also consider cost and suggest a price with a profit margin if you would like to integrate your math, science, and technology. You may want to use this material as an additional embedded assessment tool. Another way of testing their understanding and ability to explain the principles involved is to invite a class of younger students to your class so that your students can help them go through the process of developing the best toy. Regardless, I think your students will end with a better understanding of the transmission of sound energy as well as a more realistic view of the technology of improving a product.

RELATED NSTA PRESS BOOKS AND JOURNAL ARTICLES

Brown, R., and K. Boehringer. 2007. Breaking the sound barrier. *Science Scope* 30 (5): 35–39.

Cottam, M. 2006. Waves on the fly. *Science Scope* 29 (5): 22–25.

Farenga, S. and J. Ness. 2002. Sound science of the symphony: Sound intensity. *Science Scope* 25 (5): 50–53.

Palmer, D. H. 2003. Modeling the transmission of sound. *Science Scope* 26 (7): 32.

Tolman, M., and G. Hardy. 2001. Sound fun with noisy cups. *Science and Children* 38 (7): 6.

Wise, K., and M. Haake. 2007. Coffee can speakers: Amazing energy transference. *Science and Children* 44 (7): 36–40.

REFERENCES

American Association for the Advancement of Science (AAAS). 1993. *Benchmarks for science literacy.* New York: Oxford University Press.

National Research Council (NRC). 1996. *National science education standards.* Washington, DC: National Academy Press.

CHAPTER 18

HOW COLD IS COLD?

Kristin filled her glass with ice cubes from the freezer, all the way up to the top. She then filled the glass with lemonade and sat down to drink it. The day was hot and muggy and Kristin did not take long to finish her drink. When she was finished she dumped almost a full glass of ice cubes into the sink.

Kristin's father had been watching the entire scene. "You know, Krissy," he said, "You don't have to waste all of that ice. Why do you put so much ice into your glass?"

"I like my lemonade really cold," she responded, "and the more ice I put in, the colder the lemonade gets."

"Are you sure about that?" asked her dad.

"Of course," answered Kristin. "It makes sense. More cold ice makes a cold drink, well… colder."

"Maybe," said her dad "more ice might make it cool down faster, but would it really make it colder? Look! You threw away almost all of the ice!"

"It was cold enough, so I drank it all down. I can't help it if all of the ice didn't melt. Besides, if I let all of the ice melt, the lemonade would have gotten colder and colder and maybe too cold to drink. There was a lot of cold in the ice that had to go into the drink and the more ice, the more cold there was to cool the drink."

"I don't know," mumbled her dad. "Something doesn't quite make sense here. Could the lemonade get colder than the ice that's in it?"

"Well, I think so," Kristin replied cautiously. "Or maybe not. I don't really know. More ice would keep on making it colder as long as there was still ice, wouldn't it?"

"We need to do some experimenting," said her dad. "We need a hypothesis or two. It looks like we have a least a couple of questions here."

Background

Purpose

Heat and cold are often difficult concepts for children to understand. First, our everyday sloppy language gives them a predisposition to such common misconceptions as cold being a substance that moves from place to place. How often have we told others to "Close the door, you're letting the cold in?" Our colloquial language often reinforces the existence of "cold energy," when it is scientifically acceptable to refer only to heat as a form of energy that is transferred from a warmer object to a cooler one and that cold is an absence of heat.

Secondly, the story tries to set the stage for discussions and inquiry into the nature of temperature and heat and to the fact that heat exchange is the cause of what scientists call a *phase* change—when something goes from liquid to solid or vice versa. In essence this may be the students' first encounter with the laws of thermodynamics.

This story actually has its origin in a personal event that happened to my family while we were living in Africa. Our highly prized and ancient refrigerator labored daily against the oppressive 43° C degree temperature and did so valiantly just to maintain an internal temperature low enough to preserve our food. Making ice in the refrigerator was a luxury and we used it sparingly, all except our teenaged daughter who is personified as Kristin in the story. Her insistence on using large quantities of ice for her drinks led to many confrontations between Kristin and me, which are literally very close to the dialog in the story.

Related Concepts

- energy
- temperature
- thermal energy
- cooling
- solid
- phase change
- energy transfer
- heat
- melting
- freezing
- liquid
- physical change

Don't Be Surprised

Your students may well believe that cold is something that moves from colder places into warmer places and cools them off. Air conditioners blowing out cold air may add to this idea. They may believe that cold is an entity that moves much like a wind or an object. Who can blame them when we use language that emphasizes that belief? It would follow that they would believe that more ice would add to the transfer of more cold into the lemonade. Kristin thought that the more ice there was in the glass, the colder the drink would become for that very reason. They will be surprised when they find out that once a drink with ice cubes reaches a certain temperature, the continued presence of ice in the drink will not lower the temperature further.

Content Background

If you have ever filled your glass with ice to cool your drink, you will have noticed that the drink never got "too cold to drink!" Even if you forgot your drink only to return later and find the ice almost gone, you will have noticed that it is still drinkable, temperature-wise. It might certainly have been diluted and watery due to the melting of the ice, but the temperature was still within the comfort zone for drinking. How can this be when we think: There was a lot of cold in the ice that had to go into the drink and the more ice, the more cold there was to cool the drink. Should it not have gone on giving its cold to the drink, making it colder and colder?

Could it be that instead of the cold going into the drink, the heat from the drink might be going into the ice? Is this what makes ice melt? If the drink were very warm, would the ice melt faster? These wonderings can be made into testable questions and might lead you as the teacher to try out some ice experiments yourself before working with the children. Before using this story with the children I recommend that you obtain a copy of *Science Matters* by Hazen and Trefil and read Chapter 2 on energy. Their explanation of energy, in this case heat energy, will benefit you greatly and give you the confidence you need to lead your students through their inquiries. Basically here it is in a nutshell:

Thermal energy, temperature, and heat are entirely different things to a physicist. *Thermal energy* is the total amount of kinetic energy in a substance. The amount of thermal energy in a substance is determined by the amount of kinetic energy created by the amount of bouncing around of all of the molecules that make up the substance. A thermometer can only measure the thermal energy of the molecules that bounce off it and certainly not all of the molecules in a substance, but you can assume that the thermometer would register the same if it is placed anywhere in the container of the substance you are measuring.

Temperature is a human devised concept that measures the difference in this thermal energy among various objects on arbitrary temperature scales such as Fahrenheit, Celsius, or Kelvin scales. It tells us the average amount of thermal energy in any substance.

Heat is usually defined as the transfer of energy from an object that is hot to one that is cooler.

Every substance has some thermal energy in it unless it has somehow miraculously reached the temperature of absolute zero, a temperature impossible to attain even in a laboratory. Absolute zero is theoretically reached when no more thermal energy can be extracted from a substance. The larger the substance, the more thermal energy is present. Two ice cubes have twice the thermal energy as one ice cube! You might be very willing to have a small droplet of boiling water placed on your hand but not a pot of boiling water. Why not? Because there is much more heat in the pot of water than in the droplet despite the fact that they are the same temperature! Here lies the difference between heat and temperature. These ideas may seem counterintuitive to many of you, but don't let that scare you away from physics. Instead, let it intrigue you and entice you to learn more.

Thermal energy is attributed to the motion of molecules in any substance. More molecular activity means greater thermal energy and less activity means less.

So, when you heat or cool something, you are changing the activity level of its particles. Remember, heat is referred to as the energy that can be transferred from one substance to another. By adding energy to any substance, the amount of thermal energy it contains can be increased, by transferring it from the donor, such as the sun, electricity, burner, or nearby higher energy source to the receiver. Heat energy can be transferred from the warmer to the cooler by one of three methods, by conduction, radiation, or convection. You have felt the result of *conduction* when you put a spoon into a hot cup of liquid and then touched the spoon. The heat energy is transferred directly from the collision of the atoms in the liquid to the atoms in the spoon to you. You may also have felt the transfer of energy by *radiation* if you stood close to a fire or an electric heater or lamp. The energy of the heat source is in the form of infrared energy (a high energy part of the light spectrum), which in turn excites your heat sensors and you feel heat. In *convection*, the atoms in a liquid or gas set up a current of rising and falling atoms, which eventually bring everything in the substance to the same temperature. It all boils down to the laws of thermodynamics and in this case, the second law. We can summarize the Second Law of Thermodynamics by saying that heat energy moves spontaneously from a warmer area to a cooler area. An interesting phenomenon about conduction is that some substances conduct heat better than others. For instance, if you touch metal, it feels cooler than other substances in a room. This is because the heat from your body transfers more quickly to the metal and it feels cooler to you. If the metal has been in the room for a long time, it will have the same temperature as the rest of the objects in the room. Your body will be fooled into thinking that the metal is cooler when it is really not.

Kristin has formed a common misconception about energy that includes cold as a form of energy that can move from one place to another. Secondly, she has reckoned that there is an unlimited supply of this "cold" in the ice that can continue to move into the drink and continue to drop the temperature until the ice is gone. In her mind, the "cold" in the ice disappears into the drink until it is all used up. If this were true, it would be entirely possible for the drink to become colder than the temperature of the ice itself. We know this to be untrue from experience. The heat in the drink will transfer into the ice causing it to melt. The drink will never get any colder than the temperature of the ice in it. Since the ice and the drink will become the same temperature and heat can only flow from warmer to cooler and there will be no heat transfer. Only if the liquid in the drink warms to a temperature higher than the ice will heat continue to flow. In other words, heat can flow from one substance to another if there is a temperature difference between the two.

This can be tested with the aid of a thermometer and a glass of ice water. The heat in the drink changes the phase of the ice from solid to liquid by increasing the energy in the atoms in the ice as it melts. Mind you, the temperature of the ice cubes will not change as long as the cubes remain in solid form, but the heat energy from the drink will eventually change the state of water from solid (ice) to liquid. And, the resulting temperature of the ice drink will never go below that of the temperature of any given ice cube in the drink. The amount of heat in the drink, transferred to the cubes will eventually result in temperature equilibrium between the ice and the drink. When equilibrium has been reached, the temperature will go no lower. In essence, when the ice and drink have reached the same temperature, there can be no further flow of energy since everything is the same temperature. Otherwise, the law of thermodynamics that states that heat flows from the warmer substance to the cooler substance would be broken (or at least repealed!). So far, that has never happened. And I anticipate that in your work with the students, the law will be upheld.

reLaTeD ideas from NaTionaL science education standards (nrc 1996)

K–4: Properties of Objects and Materials
- Materials can exist in different states—solid, liquid and gas. Some common materials such as water, can be changed from one state to another by heating or cooling.

K–4: Light, Heat, Electricity, and Magnetism
- Heat can be produced in many ways such as burning, rubbing, or mixing one substance with another. Heat can move from one object to another.

5–8: Transfer of Energy
- Energy is a property of many substances and is associated with heat, light, electricity, mechanical motion, sound, nuclear energy and the nature of a chemical change. Energy is transferred in many ways.
- Heat moves in predictable ways, flowing from warmer objects to cooler ones until both reach the same temperature.

reLaTeD ideas from Benchmarks for science LiTeracy (aaas 1993)

K–2: The Structure of Matter
- Heating and cooling cause changes in the properties of materials. Many kinds of changes occur faster under hotter conditions.

3–5: Energy Transformations
- When warmer things are put with cooler ones, the warm ones lose heat and the cool ones gain it until they are all the same temperature. A warmer object can warm a cooler one by contact or at a distance.

6–8: Energy Transformations

- Heat can be transferred through materials by the collision of atoms or across space by radiation. If the material is fluid, currents will be set up in it that aid the transfer of heat.
- Energy appears in different forms. Heat energy is in the disorderly motion of molecules.

Using the Story With Grades K–4

This story can be used with the K–4 quite easily since Kristin's age is not clearly evident from the reading. As seen in the Standards and Benchmarks, the expectations for K–4 are that students will be able to distinguish between things that are warm and cold and to realize that when warm things are placed next to cool things, the cool things become warmer and the warm things become cooler. Also implicit in the expectations is the fact that substances can change from one state to another.

Actually, the story works better with third or fourth graders than with younger students although the discussion of the situation can give you a good insight into your students' thoughts about heat and the transfer of heat at any level. Most children by the time they come to school have had experience with ice and freezing and melting. They have also had time to develop incomplete conceptions about what is happening in this process. It might be best to focus on the melting of the ice cube for younger children and see what they already know about the phenomenon. An ice cube-melting race is a good way to involve the children and to see what they know about the process. Give each child an ice cube in a small dish and ask them to do what they can to make it melt as quickly as possible. They cannot touch it with any part of their bodies or take it to any other part of the room but are free to do anything else. Some will blow on the cube and others will wave their hands over the cube while others may move it back and forth with a pencil or pen. While you move about the room, you can ask them why they are doing what they are doing.

You may also want to administer one of probes on melting from *Uncovering Student Ideas in Science,* volumes 1 or 2 (Keeley, Eberle, and Farrin 2005; Keeley, Eberle, and Tugel 2007). "Ice Cubes in a Bag" is in volume 1 and "Ice Cold Lemonade" is in volume 2. Young children are not adept at reading thermometers and this limits their ability to conduct temperature studies. You can of course demonstrate and read the thermometer for them but this is secondhand science. It is a wonderful opportunity to teach them about temperature changes and there are digital thermometers that can be used for this purpose. Don't pass up the opportunity to have a class discussion about the story so that you can become aware of your students' ideas about heat and freezing and melting.

For the third and fourth graders the story should make sense and if they are able to use thermometers, the questions raised by Kristin and her dad can be tested. The students should discover that the temperature reaches equilibrium as soon as the liquid and the ice in the glass are at the same temperature. After this point, no matter how much ice is left in the glass, the temperature will remain the same since the flow of energy from warm to cool cannot take place since there is no difference. There will however, be a constant flow of energy from the liquid to the ice since the energy from the room will affect the liquid and the ice will absorb the excess heat as needed to maintain the equilibrium. After the ice all melts, the liquid will gradually move in the direction of the room temperature and the students will notice that the temperature will rise as it does so. Their explanations of these phenomena will provide an enlightening conversation for you and for the students. Be sure to bring the room temperature to the attention of the students by asking them how high they think the drink temperature will go. All of these findings should be put into their science notebooks and the conclusions and explanations as well. Your students might want to finish the story in their books now as well. If you need a prompt, you might ask them to predict what Kristin will say to her dad after she has experimented as they have done, backing up her response by using their findings.

Using the Story With Grades 5–8

Middle school students should have skills in reading thermometers but do not expect them truly to understand the difference between temperature as read on the thermometer and the concept of heat which is a complete abstraction. This is because in everyday life, we measure differences in energy by temperature even though energy is much different. Students therefore often confound the two. In fact the Standards documents suggest that at this age the time and effort spent in trying to teach students the difference is not worth it. Overall, the most important lesson to be learned here is that the energy moves from a higher energy source to a lower energy source and it is the heat that is transferred and not the "cold." I would also add here that it is important to realize that it takes energy to change a solid to a liquid and a liquid to a gas and that energy does not necessarily change the temperature of the substances involved. To wit, adding heat to boiling water, once it is at a full boil, does not raise the temperature of the water. It will remain at 100°C at sea level. The added energy goes into continuing the phase change from liquid to gas and will continue to do so until the liquid is entirely evaporated.

I suggest using the story with grades 5–8 as a stimulus for discussion and then for the design of experiments to find out the answer to Kristin's dilemma. The discussion will probably produce ideas that can be placed on the "our best thinking" chart and can be changed to questions and eventually hypotheses. The role of the teacher is to help focus the students' thinking on designing experiments that will answer their questions or support or not support their hypotheses.

For example, students may suggest putting thermometers in several glasses of water and then add varying amounts of ice to each one so they can monitor the temperature changes they anticipate as the ice melts. Should the containers all be made of the same material? Should the ice cubes be as much the same size as possible? Should the ice cubes come from the same tray? How should data be recorded? Will they graph them? When is the experiment over; when the ice is completely melted in all, some, one? The design depends, of course, on the hypothesis and the students should be helped to make the tests as fair as possible. Once the data are in, there may be small discrepancies. Small differences may be tempting for students to make their point. Your role might be to ask, how much difference in a measurement is significant? For example, suppose a student puts five ice cubes in one glass and one in another, and hypothesizes that the glass with five cubes will result in a lower temperature. The thermometer in the five-cube glass registers one degree cooler than the one-cube glass. One would expect if there were to be a difference, it would be more than one degree. Where could the difference come from? Perhaps the reading was faulty or perhaps the thermometers are not synchronized or perhaps the timing of the reading was different. Redoing the experiment as a class demonstration with all possibilities covered would be a reasonable solution to that problem. Remember, the stories and this book are about inquiry. There is not always a clear path to discovery and understanding. Having the students talk it all out will reap huge rewards. Then again, there may not be total agreement from all students. This is part of science too. Read the article *Teaching for Conceptual Change,* by Watson and Konicek (1991) to see how one teacher handled situations like this. During the discussion, always ask the student who makes a conclusion statement to verify the statement with evidence. Science goes deeper than opinions and your role is to remind the students of this fact. You may possess one of the computer-assisted probes that will measure the temperatures accurately and even graph the changes on the computer screen as they occur. I do not discourage the use of these but ask you to consider how your students might benefit from collecting data and doing their own graphing. Following this, the probe apparatus might solidify the concept and the students could say that the apparatus "agreed with their findings." See the subtle difference there?

I sincerely believe that at the end of the experiments and discussion, your students and perhaps, even you, will have a new and clearer idea about energy transfer and about the process in which knowledge is gained.

related NSTa Press BOOKS and JOURNaL articles

Ashbrook, P. 2006. The matter of melting. *Science and Children* 43 (4): 18–21.

Damonte, K. 2005. Heating up, cooling down. *Science and Children* 42 (9): 47–48.

Driver, R., A. Squires, P. Rushworth, and V. Wood-Robinson. 1994. *Making sense of secondary science: Research into children's ideas.* London and New York: Routledge Falmer.

Keeley, P., F. Eberle, and L. Farrin. 2005. *Uncovering student ideas in science: 25 formative assessment probes* (vol. 1). Arlington, VA: NSTA Press.

Keeley, P., F. Eberle, and J. Tugel. 2007. *Uncovering student ideas in science: 25 more formative assessment probes* (vol. 2). Arlington, VA: NSTA Press.

Line, L., and E. Christmann. 2004. A different phase change. *Science Scope* 28 (3): 52–53.

May, K., and M. Kurbin. 2003. To heat or not to heat. *Science Scope* 26 (5): 38.

Purvis, D. 2006. Fun with phase changes. *Science and Children* 43 (5): 23–25.

Robertson, W. C. 2002. *Energy: Stop faking it! Finally understanding science so you can teach it.* Arlington, VA: NSTA Press.

references

American Association for the Advancement of Science (AAAS). 1993. *Benchmarks for science literacy.* New York: Oxford University Press.

Keeley, P. 2005. *Science curriculum topic study: Bridging the gap between standards and practice.* Thousand Oaks, CA: Corwin Press.

Keeley, P., F. Eberle, and L. Farrin. 2005. *Uncovering student ideas in science: 25 formative assessment probes* (vol. 1). Arlington, VA: NSTA Press.

Keeley, P., F. Eberle, and J. Tugel. 2007. *Uncovering student ideas in science: 25 more formative assessment probes* (vol. 2). Arlington, VA: NSTA Press.

National Research Council (NRC). 1996. *National science education standards.* Washington, DC: National Academy Press.

Watson, B., and R. Konicek. 1990. Teaching for conceptual change: Confronting children's experience. *Phi Delta Kappan* 71 (9): 680–684.

CHAPTER 19
CONCLUSION

Well, how did it go? It takes a bit of letting go, doesn't it? We teachers are notorious control freaks, if we are willing to admit it to ourselves, and turning some power of control of the curriculum over to the kids is tough. After all, we are ultimately responsible for what they learn and in today's world where high stakes testing is the ultimate form of accountability it puts a lot of pressure on us—and them. And sure, I know, it takes a lot more time to teach for inquiry. The pressure to "cover" a certain amount of material is always lurking in the back of our minds. But if we think of teaching for inquiry as "uncovering" material it makes a bit more sense. By using the formative assessment strategies suggested in this book and in books that help you probe for students' understanding (Keeley, Eberle, and Farrin 2005; Keeley, Eberle, and Tugel 2007), we begin to realize that uncovering material and teaching for understanding in reality is ethically what we must do. Since students come to us with ideas already firmly entrenched and since we need to make science relevant to their lives, it makes sense to teach fewer topics and shoot for deeper understanding. Our science and math curricula have been criticized for being a mile wide and an inch deep. It has been criticized for trying to cover too many topics in too little time. If this criticism is valid, then we need to work with our students, finding out where they are and then proceeding from there. Our role then becomes one of helping them to look, without telling them what they must see. Only then can they continue to keep looking for explanations to the everyday science mysteries that spice their lives and do so without our holding their hands forever. Our role then becomes one of helping them to become less dependent upon us and more secure in using the skills we have helped them to hone. They will have to probe, through authentic inquiry, into questions that are important to the future of society.

It is our heartfelt wish that this book has helped you, in some way, to see science teaching in a different way. If it has, then we have taken another small step toward developing a scientifically literate society. The road is long and the future will look frightfully strange and new to us. But to our students who will live in that future world, it will be exciting and challenging and will require at least one common skill for those who will cope with the lightning-fast changes in their lives —the ability to maintain and use an inquiring mind.

references

Keeley, P., F. Eberle, and L. Farrin. 2005. *Uncovering student ideas in science: 25 formative assessment probes* (vol. 1). Arlington, VA: NSTA Press.

Keeley, P., F. Eberle, and J. Tugel. 2007. *Uncovering student ideas in science: 25 more formative assessment probes* (vol. 2). Arlington, VA: NSTA Press.

appendix

Some teachers who want to teach using inquiry techniques, and/or teach for conceptual change, like to have a few resources at their disposal. If there is a professional library in your school, the following books would make a fine addition. If not they can be added slowly to your personal library and will soon become dog-eared with use. All these books are available from NSTA (*www.nsta.org/store*).

American Association for the Advancement of Science (AAAS). 1993. *Benchmarks for science literacy.* New York: Oxford University Press.

Driver, R., A. Squires, P. Rushworth, and V. Wood-Robinson. 1994. *Making sense of secondary science: Research into children's ideas.* London and New York: Routledge Falmer.

Hazen, R., and J. Trefil. 1991. *Science matters: Achieving scientific literacy.* New York: Anchor Books.

Keeley, P. 2005. *Science curriculum topic study: Bridging the gap between standards and practice.* Thousand Oaks, CA: Corwin Press.

Keeley, P., F. Eberle, and L. Farrin. 2005. *Uncovering student ideas in science: 25 formative assessment probes* (vol. 1). Arlington, VA: NSTA Press.

Keeley, P., F. Eberle, and J. Tugel. 2007. *Uncovering student ideas in science: 25 more formative assessment probes* (vol. 2). Arlington, VA: NSTA Press.

Keeley, P., F. Eberle, and J. Tugel. Forthcoming. *Uncovering student ideas in science: 25 formative assessment probes* (vol. 3). Arlington, VA: NSTA Press.

National Research Council (NRC). 1996. *National science education standards.* Washington, DC: National Academy Press.

Each has a different role to play in planning for inquiry teaching. *Making sense of secondary science* is a compendium of research on children's thinking about many science concepts. In this book you will find the kinds of student preconceptions you can expect to find prevalent in your students' minds. *National Science Education Standards* is considered the base upon which all state standard documents are written. This is also true about the *Benchmarks for Science Literacy.* You will also want a copy of your own state's standards. *Science Matters* contains an overview of a broad range of science topics written for popular consumption, clearly stated and easily understood by the general population. *Science Curriculum Topic Study: Bridging the Gap Between Standards and Practice* does just what the title implies.

INDEX

Note: Page numbers in *italics* refer to charts or illustrations.

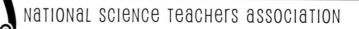